THE POWERBROKERS

THE BATTLE FOR F1's BILLIONS

ALAN HENRY

MOTORBOOKS
INTERNATIONAL

CONTENTS

First published in 2003 by Motorbooks International, an imprint of MBI Publishing Company, Galtier Plaza, Suite 200, 380 Jackson Street, St. Paul, MN 55101-3885 USA

Motorbooks International titles are also available at discounts in bulk quantity for industrial or sales-promotional use. For details write to Special Sales Manager at Motorbooks International Wholesalers & Distributors, Galtier Plaza, Suite 200, 380 Jackson Street, St. Paul, MN 55101-3885 USA.

Talk to the publisher about this book:
rob@motorbooksinternational.co.uk

ISBN 0-7603-1650-3

Printed in Hong Kong

INTRODUCTION

The huge Mercedes S-class saloon screeched to a halt inches away from the truck which it had just carved up, either inadvertently or deliberately. The truck driver wound down his window. "Are you a bleedin' half wit, or something?" he asked, directing his inquiry to the gentleman in the Mercedes. "You're a complete bloody idiot!"

Bernie Ecclestone wound down his window and looked up calmly. "You are absolutely right," he admitted in a whisper. "If I was as intelligent as you, I would be up there driving that truck, rather than down here driving this Mercedes."

This is probably my personal favourite story about Bernie. It's been circulated for years by members of his inner sanctum. Is it true? Heaven knows. But the whole point is that, to those who know the millionaire driving force behind the Formula 1 business, it is utterly and entirely believable.

I was once invited into his command centre, the grey motorhome from which he controls the F1 empire, in the paddock at Imola. His wife Slavica was with him and he was in a good mood. I think a group of us wanted to discuss with him some modifications to the information on the timing screens in the media centre. He was charm and courtesy itself. Then a phone rang, he answered and administered a right royal tongue lashing to one of his minions. Then he replaced the receiver and reverted to his good-humoured self.

"I hope I never fall out with you in a big way," I remarked nervously. "If you did, I would forgive you," he said softly, squeezing my shoulder. I trembled. It was quite an intimidating moment; I formed the strong impression that any such absolution would be conditional on some penalty, not specified at the time.

This book is unofficial. I would also claim that it is informal. Possibly irreverent, too. Neither Mr Ecclestone, nor Max Mosley, the other lynchpin of the international motor racing business, have read its text.

It is intended to pull back the curtain on the incredible business which these two men by their joint endeavours have built up over the past two decades.

You might also conclude that it is a story about lust for power, greed and avarice beyond the comprehension of mere mortals. But Ecclestone and Mosley are not the only key players in this convoluted, complex and remarkable tale. The Formula 1 team principals, whose companies have shared in the financial bonanza which has been the Grand Prix business since 1982, have also benefited hugely. This is the story of a business which is wall-to-wall with conspicuous consumption, private jets and remarkable personalities.

It is also the story of how the world's car makers finally rebelled against the way in which Ecclestone and Mosley ran the richest international sport on the planet. How bankers were deployed, fortunes won and lost. All of it is set against the backdrop of the intriguing world of Formula 1 racing, its glamour, colour and unpredictability.

Many of the people I consulted for this book probably won't want to be acknowledged – or at least identified. I would, however, like to thank my journalistic colleagues Nigel Roebuck, Maurice

Hamilton and Matt Bishop for the enjoyment and mischief we've had over the years, mulling and gossiping over the curiously compelling episodes surrounding the leading players who make up this story.

I would also like to thank F1 team principals Luca di Montezemolo, Frank Williams, Ron Dennis, Eddie Jordan and David Richards for various background briefings over the years on a variety of F1 subjects, which have helped provide the reservoir of information from which this book has evolved. My appreciation also to the staff of LAT Photographic who selected some of their tastiest images of the great men.

The same goes for Bernie and Max over the past 30 years or so. For better, for worse. For richer, for richer.

Alan Henry
Tillingham, Essex
May 2003

PREFACE

It was at the start of May 2003 that Ferrari president Luca di Montezemolo announced that the clock was ticking. His warning was stark and to-the-point. If the world's top car makers failed to reach a deal with billionaire Bernie Ecclestone over the commercial future of Formula 1 racing, then those car makers would stop negotiating and settle on starting their own breakaway series in 2008.

The deadline set by Montezemolo was 31 December 2003. The crock of gold which was Grand Prix motor racing's lucrative commercial rights pot had been the centre of protracted argument and debate for almost two years.

Now it was time for the final reckoning. Ecclestone, together with the banks who'd invested $2.1bn in loans to the now-bankrupt Kirch media empire for the purchase of a stake in the F1 entrepreneur's SLEC empire, would now have to agree to a new financial structure.

Inevitably, Ecclestone was prepared to play hard ball with his colleagues. It was the only way he knew of operating. He worked on the principle that, however strong your hand in a game of poker, it's only as good as the opposition believes it is. And he had proved consistently adroit in playing those hands to good effect over the past quarter century. "There's an offer on the table which they should not refuse," he said at the 2003 San Marino Grand Prix. "This would be more than they had ever dreamed of. The problem is that the manufacturers' concerns started when we sold SLEC to Kirch and they were worried that the sport would be dominated by pay-to-view television. That didn't happen, but now they are concerned about other things."

He was right. Montezemolo and the car makers were on the war path, determined to prise commercial control from 72-year-old Ecclestone's fingers. "We(the manufacturers) would like a solution with Mr Ecclestone and the banks," said the Italian. "If not, it will be bad, but it won't be a tragedy.

"While Bernie Ecclestone was the owner (of the rights), everyone accepted most of the arrangements. But things have changed. The car makers have a bigger presence and the cost of racing becomes bigger and bigger.

"In no other sport are the teams deprived of a share of two of the three main revenue streams – trackside advertising and ticket sales – while having to share just 47 per cent of the gross income from the TV rights."

He warned the three banks who had bought a 75 per cent share in Ecclestone's SLEC empire for a reputed $2.2bn, that if they did not agree to share more of the sport's profits their stake would shrink to nothing as the GPWC series took off.

The three creditor banks, Bayerrische Landesbank, JP Morgan and Lehman brohers, were on a hiding to nothing, he warned. "They know nothing about F1. How can we accept that?"

He added: "The simple truth is that without the car makers they cannot make a championship."

Time alone will tell how accurate those predictions will turn out to be.

01: *WHOSE GAME IS IT ANYWAY?*

Farnborough Airport, 25 miles to the west of London, on a dank morning in February 2003. A dark grey Bombardier Challenger 604 executive jet taxis out for take-off, makes a tight left turn moments after it lifts off the runway, and sets course for Bologna, in northern Italy.

Aboard the $20m aircraft are Ron Dennis, the 55-year-old chairman of the TAG McLaren group and principal of the famous McLaren Formula 1 team, and 44-year-old Martin Whitmarsh, his managing director and right-hand man. They are heading for a meeting with Luca Cordero di Montezemolo, the charismatic president of the legendary Italian car company, Ferrari.

Yet instead of taking place at the Ferrari factory, this get-together is to be staged in an anonymous building on a trading estate somewhere near Bologna. It is supposed to be secret and totally confidential.

In Formula 1 terms, this is an extraordinary gathering, almost an armistice. McLaren and Ferrari have been at loggerheads on the track for more than six seasons, each regarding the other with suspicion and mutual distrust. Harsh words have been exchanged, allegations of cheating, partiality and paranoia have been voiced, on and off the record, between the two teams in the five-star Grand Prix paddocks across the world.

Yet this extraordinary Formula 1 summit meeting is not to discuss their on-track rivalry. It is to discuss the future of Grand Prix racing – and, more specifically, to head off the prospect of this billion dollar, televised global sport tearing itself apart in public with more bitterness, acrimony and confrontation than it has experienced in more than two decades.

At the centre of the Maranello meeting was the question of Formula 1's wealth and earnings. Specifically, this high-level debate was designed to discuss the sport's income streams – a topic dominated by the fact that around $400m was now being diverted from its coffers each season.

The money was being taken out of the sport under the terms of the Concorde Agreement, an almost mystical regulatory protocol, the terms of which are guarded with religious zeal and Masonic secrecy from the outside world.

Ironically, one of the few real chinks in that protective screen surrounding the details of F1 finances was offered by Ron Dennis at the 2003 Australian Grand Prix. "To give you a round figure, just round figures," he told a media conference, "the team who wins the world championship in the preceding year – versus the team that is last in the world championship of the preceding year – receives double the amount of money.

"And the money is not huge, in round figures $22m to $11m. You might not feel that it is particularly equitable, but maybe you will be quite surprised at that spread, and (the fact) that it is relatively equalised out in increments from the tenth team to the first team."

None of this altered the bottom line reality that almost 75 per cent of the sport's earnings were being directed out of the Formula 1 business thanks to the efforts of a compact, poker-faced 73-year-old billionaire. His name was Bernie Ecclestone, the architect of Formula 1's contemporary wealth. But now – it was whispered – he had to be stopped.

This haemorrhaging of dollars could go on no longer. It was almost a matter of detail that the team principals had all signed up to the Concorde Agreement in 1997 renewing the deal for another ten years. However, getting all the signatories to toe the line had not been the work of a moment.

Three Formula 1 teams had baulked at the deal, claiming that Ecclestone was not giving them a big enough slice of the commercial cake.

Yet, back in 1997, there had been more behind-the-scenes complications than were immediately apparent at the time. Most notable was the fact that Ecclestone's business arrangements had formed the basis of a complaint to the European Union that same year by Wolfgang Eisele, the owner of a German television production company specialising in motorsports coverage.

Eisele's contract to cover truck racing had been squeezed by the deal between the Fédération Internationale de l'Automobile (FIA), the sport's international ruling body, and Ecclestone's company, International Sportsworld Communicators (ISC). It was part of Bernie's wider deal with the FIA to exploit the marketing of all non-Formula 1 areas of the sport.

Efforts to float Ecclestone's Formula One Holdings empire on the Stock Exchange in 1997 would eventually be hobbled by his ambiguous relationship with the FIA and its president, Max Mosley. This would attract the relentless and terrier-like attention of the European Union's competition commissioner, Karel van Miert, over the next couple of years.

There were also other problems. Ecclestone's secretive and private manner of operating his businesses, which had served Formula 1 so well for almost three decades, left the bankers who were involved in his float feeling rather unnerved. He was an unusual character and they did not feel totally comfortable doing business with him. Add to that the economic depression prevailing at the time, and the project never got off the launch pad.

Moreover, thinly veiled threats that the McLaren, Williams and Tyrrell teams might also add their complaints to the EU if they were not permitted to reassume their full benefits under the terms of the 1997 Concorde Agreement, after their spat with Bernie, were the last thing the diminutive tycoon really wanted. During the period they were arguing with Bernie and the FIA, they collected only the prize money accruing to them, without the additional substantial revenues from the peripheral commercial rights, notably television.

It was a vindictive and unpleasant period in Formula 1 history, with team owner Ken Tyrrell less financially able to weather the storm than the well-heeled teams of his rivals, Frank Williams and Ron Dennis. "Ken was extremely brave aligning himself with Frank and ourselves," said Dennis.

"We had the financial firepower to sit it out with Bernie, if necessary, but that was not the point. We just wanted the matter resolved."

The matter was eventually resolved when McLaren, Williams and Tyrrell signed an amended 1998 Concorde Agreement which gave them the best deal available at the time. "In restrospect, we signed under some duress," said a McLaren insider. "We should have pushed for an even better deal, which we would have done if we'd had all the information at our disposal which we subsequently acquired."

For his part, Tyrrell seemed exhausted and drained after this episode, which certainly did not help his team's chances of survival. At the start of 1998 he sold out to British American Racing for around $13m (8.2m pounds).

After Ken's death from cancer in 2001, Guildford Cathedral was packed to the rafters with friends and admirers for his Memorial Service. Neither Ecclestone nor Mosley was present.

"I love my motor racing," Tyrrell told the author in an uncharacteristically emotional conversation at the 1997 French Grand Prix, "and it pains me deeply to say that there is something very rotten at the core of this sport at the present time."

He declined to elaborate on precisely what he meant. I formed the impression he was referring to one or more of the sport's powerbrokers; if he was, this was ironic in the extreme, as Ecclestone had intervened to boost the Tyrrell coffers with a financial helping hand on more than one occasion over the preceding 25 years.

Personal relationships within the Formula 1 community can be very turbulent. It is a passionate business that relies on its participants stretching every mental, commercial and technical sinew. There is no time to let up or ease back. In such a tense, highly committed environment, it is no surprise that personal enmities run out of control.

The qualities which add up to success in this business have nothing to do with personal backgrounds either. Therefore the sport consists of what might be termed a volatile mix of disparate personalities. Small wonder that personal disdain is often what drives political jockeying as much as passionate belief.

Bear all this in mind and it should perhaps be no surprise at all that Max Mosley and Ron Dennis do not get on, a reality which injects an unpleasant edge to their quite legitimate disagreements over the manner in which Formula 1 is administered.

Think about it. Mosley is the product of an intellectual, patrician high society, well heeled and well educated. Dennis is the ultimate self-made man, the perfectionist mechanic-made-good whose relentless focus and single-mindedness built one of the most formidable F1 teams in the sport's history.

I have the impression that Mosley regards Dennis as F1's equivalent of a social climber, almost an irritating NCO who has been promoted beyond his status. I also have the impression that Dennis regards the FIA president as a dilettante, whose expansive pronouncements over the way the sport should be shaped and developed betray the fact that, despite his racing background, he has little more than an academic interest in motor racing generally. Both men, in fairness, feel that this is an exaggerated and distorted perception of their relationship. Officially, at least.

At the start of the 2003 season they clashed absolutely head-on over the issue of rule changes – and the legitimacy of the way in which those changes were imposed.

Throughout 2002 there had been acute and increasing concern that cost levels in F1 were simply no longer sustainable. The pages of motor racing history are littered with the records of teams which have gone out of business, whether through ill-fortune, bad management or a failure to adapt to changing times.

The roll-call of failure over the years is long and depressing. It includes Maserati, the Italian car maker that could not continue meeting the expense of a works F1 team and withdrew from the sport in 1958. The company is now controlled by one-time rivals Ferrari. Then there was Connaught, the British team funded by Kenneth McAlpine, a member of the civil engineering dynasty, which brought Britain's Tony Brooks his first major victory in the 1955 Syracuse Grand Prix. Overwhelmed by the cost of it all, they withdrew from racing in 1957, and some of their assets were purchased at auction by a then little-known car dealer – Bernie Ecclestone.

Next of the high profile teams to fail was Cooper, the technical trend-setters who pioneered the rear-engined Formula One technology which carried Jack Brabham to the 1959 and '60 world championships. Conservative technical thinking and lack of finance caused their demise at the end of 1968. Even Lotus, once Britain's most prestigious and respected F1 team, which dominated much of the 1960s with the legendary Jim Clark, and the 1970s with Emerson Fittipaldi and Mario Andretti, dwindled away after founder Colin Chapman's death in 1982 and finally went bust in 1994.

Despite these high-profile failures, Grand Prix racing had thrived for three decades through to the end of the 1990s, delivering television viewing figures which seemed to go racing onwards and upwards without any prospect of a glitch. Like Icarus, however, they eventually flew too close to the sun. Their wings melted and by 2001 they were dipping, if not exactly plummeting.

During these golden years, Formula 1 costs had also rocketed. In 1994, the Jordan team spent just under $5m (3.18m pounds) with specialist Brian Hart on a V10 engine programme which carried them to fifth place in the Constructors' Championship.

A decade later, leasing a Cosworth V10 capable of achieving the same result would cost $18m (11.46m pounds). There seemed no limit to the huge multi-million dollar companies that were prepared to invest in these high-tech teams in a bid to grab a slice of the global television viewership cake. Then came the economic downturn at the start of the new millennium and, by the end of 2002, the sport was facing a crisis.

In fairness to Ecclestone, he had warned the competing teams over several years to keep an eye on their cost base. Ironically, the man who was taking most of the money out of the sport could see that his team-owning colleagues were heading for potential trouble. And the sport's appeal was also being buffeted by the seemingly interminable domination of Michael Schumacher and the Ferrari team, which had rattled off a hat-trick of world championships between 2000 and 2002.

Yet there was another, more immediate, dimension to the concerns of both Dennis and Whitmarsh as their aeroplane started to descend towards Bologna airport, over the flatlands of the Emilia Romagna. The world's top automobile manufacturers were pressing for a say in how the Formula 1 business was run, and for a stake in its revenues. Not to suck out of the business, but to ensure a more equitable share of Grand Prix racing's income amongst the participating teams. And they were prepared to eyeball it out with Ecclestone to get their way.

The car makers' dissent was first signalled towards the end of 2001. At a meeting in Geneva on 27 November, a new Dutch-registered company, GPWC Holding BV (standing for Grand Prix World Championship), was established with Fiat chief Paolo Cantarella named as its chairman. The first thing the manufacturers did was to send a message to the Kirch Group, the German media empire which had purchased 75 per cent of Ecclestone's Formula 1 empire, warning that if it did not increase the share of F1 commercial rights payable to the competing teams, they would press ahead with their own independent racing series from 2008.

As things stand, the top ten teams share 47 per cent of the television revenue generated by the F1 World Championship, with the 53 per cent balance split between Kirch (75 per cent) and Bambino Trust, acting for Ecclestone's SLEC empire (25 per cent). In fairness, the teams' share is taken out of the gross commercial rights pot, whereas the Ecclestone/Kirch share has to absorb the transport, setting-up and running costs of the F1 TV operation – as the teams did not want to take the risk on that.

Ecclestone also has a monopoly on the freight transportation to races outside Europe. Beyond a fixed minimum of around 20 personnel, three cars and 15 tonnes of freight, the teams have to pay Ecclestone to transport their equipment. No options, no alternatives. He has a monopoly on the deal.

"In fact," said Dennis, "the bottom line amount distributed to the teams is much nearer 23 per cent (of the total income of the F1 business) than 47 per cent – taking into account all commercial resources we can understand and quantify." What complicates the whole issue, of course, and has led to a degree of burning resentment amongst the teams, is that all the circuit revenue – advertising, the extremely expensive "Paddock Club" for the sport's high rollers, and trackside signage – is controlled by Allsport Management, run by millionaire entrepreneur Paddy McNally.

Allsport pays Ecclestone's companies a $50m annual licensing fee out of revenues believed to be in the region of $130m. The teams get none of this. Thus while the competitors share a maximum of around $200m between them during an average season, Ecclestone and his associates earn at least twice that figure. It was not a situation that could endure on an open-ended basis.

There is also preferential treatment for Ferrari, of course. In recognition of the fact that Formula 1 is absolutely nothing without the Prancing Horse, Maranello receives a separate 4 per cent slice of television income – which comes out of Bernie's 53 per cent – and more in the event of Ferrari becoming a publicly quoted company.

Moreover, the world's major car manufacturers have proposed a $50m one-off advance bonus to Ferrari to help persuade them to line up behind the planned breakaway GPWC series in 2008. This news shocked some of the smaller F1 teams, who were aware that the famous Italian team would continue to receive that extra 4 per cent from the sport's commercial revenues, as they do under Bernie Ecclestone's current regime.

They were deeply surprised when it emerged over the 2003 San Marino GP weekend that Ferrari would be paid this additional bonus. Yet many F1 insiders believe that such a bonus will be necessary to guarantee Ferrari's long-term future health at a time where there is much speculation about the prospect of the Maranello firm becoming a public company. Yet the money was intended to come out of a "special fund" provided by the car makers in a bid to get Ferrari onside. It was not coming from the teams' proposed income stream.

In what was perceived as a direct challenge to Ecclestone's iron grip on the sport's levers of power, GPWC was now going to offer the teams – which collectively invest more than $1 billion each year participating in the F1 World Championship – as much as 85 per cent of the commercial rights pot.

BMW, DaimlerChrysler, Fiat, Ford and Renault were the founders of the GPWC, with Toyota hopefully joining later. A joint press release from them stated that the aims of the new series were to "improve in a substantial way the financial benefits of the participating teams and to guarantee absolute economic transparency."

The board of directors of the new company included Cantarella, Patrick Faure of Renault, Burkhard Goeschel (BMW), Jurgen Hubbert (DaimlerChrysler) and Wolfgang Reitzle (Ford/Jaguar). Within five months of GPWC's foundation, the group were stunned to hear that Kirch had failed, with a debt mountain that made it the biggest corporate failure in Germany since the Second World War.

"The bottom line was that Kirch bought three sets of 25 per cent shareholdings in SLEC for around $2.2bn," said one banker. "That money was loaned to them by three banks, JP Morgan, Lehman Brothers and the much smaller Bayerische Landesbank. Now you might have *assumed* that everybody involved would have read the articles of association of SLEC, the company that they were buying.

"The evidence suggests that in some cases the due diligence was insufficient, and all they'd purchased were three minority stakes in a business plus the rights to see the accounts, attend board meetings and receive 75 per cent of the income from the business. If there was any."

However, before any of the 75 per cent income can be distributed, provision for paying both interest and capital off the original $1.4bn, ten-year bond, launched on Ecclestone's behalf in 1999, has to be allowed for. That meant that while the teams were duly receiving their 47 per cent of the television revenue, split ten ways, the Ecclestone side of the equation was taking little if anything out of the equation.

Neither are the three deeply concerned banks. "The real problems for those banks is the fact that they are stuck with an investment they don't want, and one which could be worth nothing by the end of the 2007 season," said one City of London insider. "As long as they show the investment on their books as valued (collectively) at around $2bn, they are alright in theory. But if they take the loss, it's not going to look very good at all. I understand the car manufacturers have already offered to buy SLEC, but the banks are very nervous about selling at a loss because of the impact it could have on their balance sheets."

You might be forgiven for thinking that this implies Ecclestone is unfairly opportunistic. Not one bit of it, according to City sources. "Dealing in Formula 1 is really a case of 'buyer beware,'" said one. "Bernie is very straight, very direct, but you'd better make sure you ask him the right questions.

"If you've been seduced by the glamour, rock and roll of Formula 1 - and you don't ask the right questions – then more fool you. Formula 1 is played to Big Boy's rules and Bernie knows that. Nobody is going to look after you if you don't ask the right questions."

Kirch's bankers initially offered the car makers a 30 per cent stake in their business, which they optimistically claimed was worth as much as $2.4 billion. But it was only on the condition that the manufacturers scrapped their plans for a separate series, and swore unconditional allegiance to the existing Formula 1 infrastructure. It was not hard to detect the guiding hand of Ecclestone on the tiller at this point, for the bankers were very keen to get out of the debris of the Kirch empire. Yet Ecclestone had already enjoyed his personal pay-day and could afford to take a strategic view of the mounting chaos.

The car makers were not going to be bounced into precipitate decisions. They felt they held all the cards. Despite this, there was acute scepticism amongst some teams. "Some of these car company bosses are on an ego trip," remarked one Formula 1 team principal. "You would have thought they could work out that, in the current economic environment, what Formula 1 needs more than ever is long-term stability. Nobody seriously believes they have a hope of starting their own series. It's just designed to put pressure on Bernie and Kirch."

At the time, Martin Whitmarsh had observed: "Clearly any uncertainty surrounding Formula 1 television rights is something the teams are aware of and concerned about. The teams enjoy some of the income derived from those rights, but we now believe that the car manufacturers' commitment to backing an alternative championship from 2008 provides a degree of stability to the current negotiations."

Cynics, of course, brushed this aside, pointing out that DaimlerChrysler owned 40 per cent of TAG McLaren, and that Whitmarsh was just towing the GPWC line. But as Dennis wryly remarked in another context: "Or you could say, we have a 60 per cent stake in TAG McLaren." It was easy to see both implied viewpoints.

Whitmarsh also pointed out: "In a worst case scenario – Kirch selling to somebody not committed to exploiting the Formula 1 rights in a professional manner – then the manufacturers will organise the commercial rights to an alternative Grand Prix-style series."

Given that the offer exists from the manufacturers and is on the table, the Formula 1 teams certainly had an alternative scenario in place in the longer term. Dennis warned: "Anybody not taking GPWC seriously is making a big mistake. Its long-term programme is driven on the basis of what is best for the competing teams."

Ironically, the most powerful and influential man in the GPWC lobby was Montezemolo, the man who carried the responsibility for the Fiat group's Formula 1 presence in the form of Ferrari. In days gone by, it used to be said that Enzo Ferrari kept world champions waiting at his beck and call outside his offices at Maranello. This was just to make the point that he was the man who called the shots in what had, even by the late 1950s, become a sacred shine to those obsessed with powerful cars and the narcotic glamour of motor racing.

The Commendatore certainly had a powerful personality, although whether he had great charm is still a matter for some debate amongst those who knew him well, even years after his death. Montezemolo adds punctuality to both that power and charisma. Much of his presence undoubtedly stems from the fact that, for much of his career, he was regarded as the anointed one, the keeper of the flame first lit by Enzo Ferrari when the first sports car to carry his name made its race debut in an event at Piacenza back in 1947.

At 55, Montezemolo is more than just the public face of Ferrari. He is a distinguished personality in his own right in Italian sporting circles. His two spells at Ferrari from 1974 to 1976, and from 1992 to the present day, surround jobs with Fiat and Cinzano, running Italy's first America's Cup yachting challenge, and organising the staging of the 1990 World Cup in Italy.

Yet when Michael Schumacher won the 2000 Japanese Grand Prix, thereby clinching the first Ferrari driver's championship for 21 years, it was a momentous day for Bologna-born Montezemolo, who originally left Rome University in 1971 with a law degree. "For me, getting the Drivers' World Championship back to Ferrari was maybe the biggest professional satisfaction of my life," he insists. "Sure enough, I won the title in 1975 as a team manager, but that was different. I was not chairman and managing director then. Enzo Ferrari was still there."

Yet while Montezemolo talks with great passion about cars, drivers and famous races long past, he also has a keen appreciation of Ferrari's position at the epicentre of Formula 1 politics and commerce. He knows that Ferrari is the sport's biggest box office draw and knows how to harness that influence to get his way. Interestingly, Ecclestone and Mosley were quick to realise that reality in the early 1980s when the first Concorde Agreement was being forged.

Keeping Ferrari on side was absolutely crucial to gaining access to the sport's commercial purse strings. Ecclestone, who defers publicly to few individuals, was also clever enough to mind his manners whenever he went to confer with Enzo Ferrari. On one occasion Mosley recalled him arriving at Maranello and quickly removing his tinted spectacles, similar to those worn by the Commendatore.

"Wouldn't want him to think I was taking the piss," whispered Bernie to his accomplice.

Luca was a different proposition altogether. He knew the ins and outs of how Bernie worked, from his days as Ferrari team manager.

He was less romantically bound up in the Ferrari legend than the Commendatore, deploying a more worldly and pragmatic approach to dealing with the man who holds the commercial rights to Formula 1 – Ecclestone.

In 2001 he warned Ecclestone, who was then concentrating on developing digital pay-to-view TV coverage of Formula 1, that he would have nothing to do with any deal that might shift the emphasis of Formula 1 television coverage from terrestrial channels to a pay-to-view basis, something which Kirch clearly seemed to have in mind.

Luca was concerned that the high-profile sponsors in the F1 business might be frightened away unless Ecclestone's claimed terrestrial TV viewing figures of around 5 billion viewer/minutes per year could be sustained. It was hardly surprising. With an operating budget in 2003 conservatively estimated at around $500m, the investments of Vodafone ($100m), Philip Morris ($170m) and Shell ($90m) certainly needed some justification.

In the end, he need not have worried. F1's digital coverage never took off and was withdrawn at the end of 2002.

By the time Dennis and Whitmarsh arrived to meet him, they also knew full well that Montezemolo was on their side when it came to challenging Ecclestone on the question of increased income for the teams. He was prepared to use the leverage available from the GPWC threat and had already made it very clear that while Ferrari was prepared to sign up for cost-cutting measures to help the sport in time of crisis, this had to be linked to a better income flow from Ecclestone.

"I think that Bernie has done a great job for Formula 1 over the years, and I well remember him at the constructors' meetings back in 1973 when I first joined Ferrari as assistant team manager to Enzo Ferrari," he said. "Things were different then. I remember being sent as an annual ritual by Mr Ferrari to Monza to demand more passes and more starting money for the Italian Grand Prix, or else he wouldn't send his cars.

"Bernie changed all that and did much to market the Formula 1 business over the last two decades. But, as with everything, life changes. We, the teams, get not one penny of the circuit advertising or the ticket sales. If the grandstands at the circuits are full or empty, it doesn't make the slightest bit of difference for the teams. So we have to change this, because the future of Formula 1, as ever, depends on the balance between the large and the small teams."

He then took a direct swipe at Ecclestone, saying: "The issue is not, as some people have said, what we might or might not pay Michael Schumacher, but how much income permeates down to the likes of Sauber, Jordan and the smaller teams. And as things stand at the moment, not enough gets down to them to ensure that they can survive."

The most recent Formula 1 commercial crisis had been triggered in November 2001 when Alain Prost's team filed for bankruptcy in the French courts. Prost, four times a world champion behind the wheel, pledged that he would fight his way back to solvency and save the team which had a 250-strong workforce at its state-of-the-art factory at Guyancourt, near Paris.

There were no takers. Two months later, Prost's dream of building a Formula 1 team which would rival his success as a driver lay in tatters, when a French court ordered that his company should be put into liquidation. Hopes that a fresh injection of capital from outside investors might save the day were dashed after weeks of speculation, leaving Prost Grand Prix with unmanageable debts of $25m (16m pounds) and its staff out of work. Prost had filed an entry for the 2002 World Championship, which opened with the Australian Grand Prix in Melbourne on 3 March. But he never made it.

"The poor guy, I am so sorry to hear the news," said then Jaguar team principal Niki Lauda, who beat the Frenchman to the 1984 World Championship by the smallest ever margin – half a point – when they were team-mates at McLaren.

"His team went wrong at the wrong time. If you do not perform and the economy is strong, there is a chance to fight your way out of trouble. If you do not perform and there is a recession, you are in trouble.

"Normally in Formula 1 it is possible to ride the storm. But private teams such as Prost, which do not have a major motor manufacturer behind them, have a double problem. The works teams have an easier time that the independents."

Yet, for all that, even Ferrari had problems looming on the horizon. By the start of 2003, despite a massive budget rumoured by some to be in the order of $600m, it seemed that the death of Gianni Agnelli, Fiat's patriarch, might have long-term effects on the company's financial strength. In some ways, Agnelli provided the symbolism that helped secure the Ferrari legend. But now outsiders were involved.

In June 2002, the powerful Italian investment bank Mediobanca had purchased a 34 per cent stake in Ferrari for around $772m (490m pounds). Mediobanca then sold off part of that stake, 10 per cent to the German Commerzbank and 2 per cent to Banca Popolare Emilia Romagna. Enzo Ferrari's second son Piero retained his 10 per cent stake.

Now it was being suggested that too much of the team's road car profits in 2002 was directed to help fund the Formula 1 team. In future, the new part-owners wanted it capped at a fraction of that amount. Previously, Montezemolo had addressed the question of the financial balance inside Ferrari by saying: "We are owned 90 per cent as a financial investment by Fiat Holding Company. We are not owned by Fiat Automotive sector. We are, thank God, totally independent in terms of cash flow."

No longer. And with a manufacturing base of 4500 road cars, Ferrari had precious little resources to fall back on if its Formula 1 income from sponsorship and television rights was materially dented. Even Porsche, with 60,000 cars produced per year, had baulked at the costs of being involved in Formula 1. Without more income from the Grand Prix money machine, Ferrari's position clearly risked becoming seriously weakened over the next few years.

"There is no question, Formula 1 is very expensive, but there is nothing new there," said Montezemolo just before Christmas 2002. "There is also no question that we have to invest a lot of money to be competitive, but when I hear (people talk about) 'all the unbelievable budget, because (we) have Fiat behind us,' I have to say again that Fiat is not amongst the five most important sponsors of Ferrari.

"But if we put together all the investment in electronics, chassis and engines of other teams, these can't be compared with Ferrari. We can make the comparison between the budget of Ferrari and these teams, plus their engine manufacturer."

Then he offered a stark warning: "If you consider that the three most important technology and industrial countries in the world are in crisis – USA, Germany and Japan – and if you consider that media advertising has been in crisis for two years, then you can imagine that sponsors can be in crisis. You can do advertising and sponsorship; you cannot do only sponsorship without advertising."

It seemed like a parable for Formula 1's troubled times.

A week after the secret meeting between Dennis, Whitmarsh and Montezemolo near Bologna, Ecclestone attended the Geneva Motor Show, where he had a private meeting with members of GPWC. The meeting made little positive headway. The manufacturers were determined on their chosen course. It even emerged that they had appointed a London-based firm of headhunters to find the necessary high-profile personality who could do for GPWC what Ecclestone had done for Formula 1 over the past three decades.

On the face of it, this looked a hopelessly optimistic challenge. At this point, and demonstrating his matchless political savvy, Ecclestone made an offer to the F1 teams. He suggested that his own family trust, SLEC, would buy back the 75 per cent stake owned by the banks. It would then be floated on the stock market, enabling the teams to gain a stake in their own business.

But this was contingent on the teams signing up for an extension to the Concorde Agreement from 2008 to 2015. This prompted Montezemolo to accuse Ecclestone in words of one syllable of being greedy.

"He made huge amounts of money, becoming one of the richest men in Britain, but he wanted too much for himself," Montezemolo said. "It is his biggest mistake. Now the car manufacturers are not prepared to fund the banks. They prefer to have it in their own pockets. Without us in 2008, the banks will own 100 per cent of nothing.

"We are preparing a new championship without banks, without Bernie, and with a far bigger cake. It's not blackmail. It's our right to expand."

Ecclestone responded with a low punch. "If Luca is so clever, how comes he hasn't solved the problems at Fiat?" he fumed. Even Bernie knew that was not the point. But it was just the sort of provocative, off-the-cuff remark that he had made his speciality.

On a more serious note, he warned against anybody who might be thinking of breaching the existing terms of the Concorde Agreement, saying: "If the teams or manufacturers do anything to induce a breach of contract, we will sue the hell out of them. Writs will fall like leaves in autumn."

He added: "The GPWC lot are just holding out to take control of Formula 1 without paying for it. Formula 1 doesn't need this trouble." Ecclestone was clearly spoiling for a fight. A master poker player, he was confident he held all the cards. Or, at the very least, that GPWC really could not be *totally* certain what cards the pocket-sized billionaire held in the palm of his hand.

In parallel with all this commercial behind-the-scenes manoeuvring, Mosley was fielding an inevitable barrage of flak from the competing teams over the 2003 technical and cost-reducing rule changes. He was unapologetic, citing the failure of the Arrows team in January 2003, and the financial problems facing Jordan and

Minardi, as the clear justification for a draconian package to keep costs in check.

It was precisely the sort of confrontation he relished, and when both Ron Dennis and Frank Williams accused him of "being hostile to the manufacturers who will consistently support Formula 1", he rounded on them with a familiar, well-practised mantra.

"You are ignoring history as well as business reality," he told the two team principals. "Both your engine suppliers (BMW and Mercedes) have been in and out of Formula 1 and other branches of motorsport over and over again.

"The fact that they say they would like to invest in Formula 1 does not change that. They are answerable to their shareholders, not to the sport. They can, and will, leave whenever it suits them. That is not a criticism, it is a statement of fact."

In an attempt to ram home his point, Mosley added: "You must remember that a car manufacturer is not spending its shareholders' money to support motorsport, it is spending it to win and sell more product.

"We are currently seeing a money-spending contest with one manufacturer – and it's not Ferrari – employing upwards of 1000 people and virtually unlimited resources in an attempt to win the FIA Formula 1 World Championship." This might well be Toyota, then again it could have been Mosley grandstanding for theatrical effect.

He continued: "There is nothing wrong with that, the rules certainly do not prohibit it. But we cannot prevent that manufacturer stopping tomorrow if, for example, its shareholders stage a revolt. In trying to make sure that Formula 1 can continue irrespective of the number of major manufacturers involved, we are not being hostile, merely realistic."

Mosley then moved on to capitalise on the fact that both Paolo Cantarella of Fiat and Wolfgang Reitzle of Jaguar had been removed from their jobs in the 18 months since GPWC was first mooted. Emphasising the fragile and transitory role of these executives, he added: "The manufacturers contribute a lot and we must continue to do all we can to encourage them to stay. But we must never be so naive as to believe we can rely on them."

Then came the killer blow. "It would be folly to allow Formula 1 to be at the mercy of personnel and policy changes in the major manufacturers."

Mosley continued to reiterate his insistence that recently discussed, long-term cost-cutting changes must be implemented without delay to help the smaller teams.

"Unlike a manufacturer, an independent team cannot just stop racing, because to do so would be to close its business," he said. "Thus the way to guarantee the long-term health and stability of the Championship is to make sure there is a solid group of independent teams which do not depend on the presence of the manufacturers for their survival.

"We can rely on the independent teams. We cannot rely on the manufacturers."

Less than a month after issuing this warning, Ford's catastrophic financial results prompted Wall Street to slash its profits forecast for the Detroit car giant. Having lost $6.5 billion during 2001/02, Ford claimed its automotive arm would make $1.2 billion in 2003, but the analysts remained sceptical.

This was just the sort of risk Mosley seemed concerned about. In his view, it would only take an aggressive accountant to slash a red line through the entry on the balance sheet marked "Formula 1" and that would be the end of another car company's involvement. Yet the car makers believed Mosley was missing the point. The popularity of Formula 1 was such, they claimed, that it had become an almost indispensable global marketing tool. They were in for the long haul in a way they had never been in the past.

Yet Formula 1 was extremely expensive – and they believed they had a right to a say in the way it was run, and the way in which its revenues were distributed, in exchange for their massive and continuing investments. In February 2003, Renault vice president Patrick Faure further endorsed the GPWC standpoint, reiterating the point that the status quo was certainly not an option.

"We have finalised a solution for the future, with an organisational agreement to replace the Concorde Agreement in 2008," he said. "We have appointed Goldman Sachs to talk to the banks and Bambino Trust to see if we can find a compromise solution. If we could, I think it would be extremely good for Formula 1, otherwise we will wait for 2008 and then we'll launch our championship."

I challenged Faure directly on this. Surely, I suggested, there was not a single Formula 1 team principal who, in his heart of hearts, truly believed that GPWC was going to get off the ground. It was a negotiating ploy, nothing more.

He smiled as he replied: "There are so many occasions in life when people do not believe things will happen and then they happen. I can promise you now that we will explain to the teams our business plan and I have the feeling that things are very clear.

"I hope we will have a compromise. But one thing is very important. The money has to go to all the teams, on an equal and transparent basis. GPWC or whatever, that's the way it's going to happen in the future.

"There has been the first era of Formula 1, now there will be another. We are happy to keep Bernie as CEO, but the majority of the money generated by Formula 1 has to go to the teams.

"Everything else is negotiable. But on this we will not compromise. We need this sport to be paid for by the revenues it generates."

In April 2003 the teams signed a memorandum of agreement at a GPWC meeting which amounted to an agreement in principle to support the new series, although it was far from the cast-iron commitment which some might have expected.

The question of Ferrari being rewarded with an additional 35m pound payment for aligning itself with the GPWC also raised eyebrows amongst the other teams who have become reconciled to

Ecclestone making an extra payment of 4 per cent of the F1 revenues out of his own 53 per cent share under the present regime.

"Nobody would argue against the fact that Ferrari have a unique place in the history of F1 and the awareness of Ferrari is greater than that of any other team," said David Richards, the BAR-Honda team principal. "But if we are starting a new regime we need a fresh debate. We need fully to understand how this will all work."

Whether GPWC offers Ferrari the most advantageous long-term answer was another matter altogether. At a recent meeting David Richards described the proposed GPWC business plan as "flawed and naive." It was an observation that caused a degree of tension amongst the car manufacturers, and raised a smile from Ecclestone when he was told.

Ecclestone had yet another negotiating card up his sleeve, however, his behind-the-scenes support for the US CART series which was now under the sympathetic and efficient stewardship of his old collaborator, Chris Pook.

It was increasingly being rumoured that Ecclestone would take a stake in CART sometime during 2003, and this speculation was heightened when David Clare, one of Bernie's most trusted and longest serving lieutenants, took over as CART chairman alongside Pook late in 2002.

Pook, who had presided over the introduction of a "one engine" CART formula for 2003 and '04, using methanol-fuelled 2.65-litre turbo Cosworth V8s, emphasised that his long-term plans would see Formula 1 and CART becoming more closely aligned in the future. And that meant 3-litre V10 engines running on pump petrol.

"We have to align ourselves more and more with the automobile industry as it exists today," said Pook. "A V10 is sophisticated and you'll see that the world's (car) manufacturers are moving towards V10s.

"At the Detroit Motor Show, Ford made a big issue about building a V10. You've got Volkswagen making V10s and others are coming out."

The unspoken advantage with a V10 was the fact that the seven engine manufacturers building V10s for Formula 1 could get more mileage from their investment if a CART application also beckoned.

More significantly, the spectre of Bernie bringing Formula 1 and CART together as a truly global, one-class, single-seater formula could be seen shimmering on the distant horizon.

That way, he could create an unstoppable international racing formula that the car makers might be begging to sign up for, possibly without having to dissipate his income by cutting them in on a share.

At the time this volume went to press, there was still plenty of mileage left to run in the stand-off between Ecclestone and the car makers. Yet it would have been a bold person indeed who would bet against Ecclestone getting his way at the end of the day. Or at least cutting a deal with the manufacturers that would see him remaining in overall control of the game.

So whose game was it anyway? We know whose it *was* but whether Ecclestone can hang onto it in the future depends on the car makers' determination and ability to continue offering a united front.

Even money, at best.

02: LAMBS TO THE SLAUGHTER

During his fledgling years running the Brabham Formula 1 team in the mid-1970s, Bernie Ecclestone once said to the author in a moment of frustration: "If I didn't really love this business, I would invest my money somewhere which offered a better return."

With the benefit of almost 30 years' hindsight, one is bound to murmur politely: "Like what?" A high-interest Liquid Helium bonus account at his High Street bank? I think not, somehow. By any standards there now seems a certain piquant irony to those remarks. Bernie, 73 years old at the time of writing these words in early 2003, has now probably become the single richest individual in Britain amongst those whose fortune has been accumulated by their own endeavour.

About five years ago, when he first appeared in the popular newspapers' Rich Lists, as being worth many millions of pounds, Max Mosley remarked wryly: "I think the people who compile these lists may be confusing net worth with annual income."

That was another perceptive observation. Mosley's implicit point was the singularly obvious truism that unravelling the business affairs of a shrewd, hard-nosed international tycoon is not simply a question of going to Companies House and paying for a copy of the Ecclestone company accounts.

The story of international motor racing over the past generation is one of stupendous success, with riches beyond the imagination accruing to a small group of highly motivated entrepreneurs who hitched their fortunes to Ecclestone's rising star. It took Ecclestone just over 25 years to come from running a used car dealership in a south London suburb to rank as the sixth richest man in Britain, reputedly worth 3.83bn pounds ($5.4bn). And he reached this spectacular level of business success by having the foresight to exploit and understand the television coverage potential offered by Grand Prix motor racing.

In his position as president of Formula 1 Management and Formula 1 commercial rights holder, he is the most powerful man in world motor racing. Some people would claim he is even the most powerful man in world sport.

Compact, trim and hyperactive, he knows everybody and everything that goes on within F1, operating his empire at the races from a discreet silver grey motorhome in the paddocks across Europe. Yet even the most astute entrepreneur can sometimes back a loser. At one point Ecclestone had seemed poised to get richer still, if digital television coverage in Europe had really taken off at the turn of the century.

He was standing poised to reap the benefits of $64m (40m pound) investment in a "portable" television studio which was transported round the world, simply to handle the digital coverage. Yet it never happened.

The number of fans prepared to pay 12 pounds ($19) per race for the ingenious camerawork and behind-the-scenes coverage never produced their credit cards in the numbers required to make the operation economically feasible.

His F1 administration organisation, together with FOCA Communications, at one time employed such a large number of personnel that he purchased two BA146 120-seater jet airliners to transport them to the European races.

Unfortunately, Ecclestone found himself having to make 300 of his workforce redundant just before Christmas 2002, rationalising the failure of F1 digital coverage by saying that it was a good product, just not the product that the public wanted. By March 2003, both the 146s were on the market.

The history of F1 over the past two decades is also effectively the story of what amounts to a secret society, whose rules and conventions are guarded with a confidentiality which many people find is quite amazing for a high-profile international sport. Moreover, those who pry too closely into the financial structures of the sport are discreetly rebuffed.

Even those senior F1 team principals who one gets the feeling would be fundamentally willing to spill the beans on the sport's finances, clam up when it actually comes to explaining how the income is shared out.

Go to Wimbledon for the men's finals and you will find out from the programme precisely how much in prize money is paid out to the leading performers. Buy a programme for the British Grand Prix and you will find that none of these juicy financial details are shared with the paying public.

There are many outside the F1 paddock who believe Ecclestone has hijacked F1 for his own devices, creating a cash cow which has delivered billions of dollars for his companies over the past two and a half decades. His critics say he has lived off the back of the compliant teams for too long, his efforts assisted by another shrewd key player, his former right-hand man and legal advisor.

That is Mosley, who in 1991 became president of the governing body, the FIA. For all the sport's apparent codified formality, Ecclestone and Mosley have effectively ruled the sport through the force of their strong personalities. F1 has always been a highly political business, but to enter a Grand Prix paddock in the first decade of the New Millennium is to be transported into an exclusive private fiefdom where Ecclestone and his minions rule by a mixture of mutual acquiescence and subtle intimidation.

Team principals have been known to stand in line outside the grey motorhome to get extra passes for their guests from him. This is one specific area which absolutely infuriates the team bosses and, more recently, has come increasingly to annoy the car makers as they consider their plans to stage their own championship from 2008 onwards.

"This business has been run like a corner shop for far too long," said one senior car company executive in 2003. "Bernie was the right man for his time, but F1 has outgrown this autocratic, hands-on approach. This is one thing which absolutely has to change, even if Bernie stays on in the same role."

Whatever pretence at democracy there might be in F1, Ecclestone's dynamic presence and ability to coax people into seeing his point of view – perhaps with a healthy slice of intimidation thrown in – remain the driving force behind the sport's evolution.

In the immediate post-war era, international motor racing was an uncoordinated, almost informal sport which was populated by more than a handful of wealthy team owners. It was the era of Enzo Ferrari, industrialist Tony Vandervell, John Cooper, whiskey heir Rob Walker and Colin Chapman. In engineering terms they were honest artisans with the occasional touch of genius, but shrewd businessmen who knew a deal when they saw it. The sport had a basic structure to it, almost a democracy.

Yet if you were a critic, you would say it was fragmented and badly organised. If he felt so inclined, Enzo Ferrari might not send his cars to the British Grand Prix, usually citing an Italian metal workers' strike as his reason. The deferential media would never seek to question his excuse. The reality, of course, was that he knew when his cars would be beaten, and a disappointed UK viewing public would pay the price for that absence. As Luca di Montezemolo recalled, as late as 1974 he could screw more money and other benefits from the Italian Grand Prix organisers by threatening that Ferrari would not turn up.

The sport has admittedly been popular with the masses for five decades now. The British Grand Prix regularly attracted crowds in the order of 100,000, whether it was being staged at Silverstone, Brands Hatch or Aintree. Yet the money involved was minimal. The first post-war British Grand Prix had been held at Silverstone on 2 October 1948, when the admission charge was 7s 6d – about 37p (60 cents) in today's currency and worth about 10 pounds ($16) in terms of 2003 purchasing power. The works Maserati team was paid significant starting money, even though the Italian squad did not turn up until after practice was over.

By contrast, the British private racers, including independent Maserati competitor Bob Ansell, had to pay an entry fee of 20 pounds (the equivalent of 450 pounds – $720 – today) in order to compete in this prestigious event. There is also an interesting financial perspective to all this. When the foundations of Silverstone were – literally – laid in the Second World War, the records of the British Racing Drivers' Club show that Mowlem, the civil engineers, charged the Royal Air Force 1.127m pounds to construct the runways and five associated aircraft hangars.

Ecclestone would race at the 1951 British Grand Prix meeting. This was a seminal moment in Formula 1 history, but not because of the achievements of the man in the immaculate Cooper-Norton Formula 3 car. No, Silverstone '51 was the day that Enzo Ferrari's name became associated with victory in a round of the Formula 1 World Championship. Froilán González, the tubby but immensely strong Argentine driver, took the 4.5-litre V12-engined Ferrari 375 past the chequered flag first, beating his compatriot Juan Manuel Fangio's supercharged Alfa Romeo in the process.

It was regarded as a turning point in motor racing history. It mattered not that Silverstone was still identifiably a Second World

War aerodrome, that the makeshift track layout was delineated by oil drums and that the spectators were penned into their viewing enclosures by little more than a protective rope strung out on the edge of the circuit.

By any standards, this was a compelling sport, spiced with genuine danger for the generation who had grown up beneath the sunny skies bisected by the vapour trails of the Battle of Britain just a decade earlier. This was also an era in which good manners and suitably deferential behaviour were still key hallmarks of our society.

John Bolster, the technical editor of *Autosport* magazine, understandably concentrated much of his BBC commentating focus on the performance of the new all-British BRM V16s. After interviewing Reg Parnell, who finished fifth despite suffering intense agony from burns on his feet caused by acute overheating in the car's poorly ventilated cockpit, Bolster commented: "In conclusion, I would like to thank Reg Parnell for consenting to give me a broadcast interview when he was in great pain from his burns."

Half a century later, anyone wanting to conduct a "broadcast interview" with any F1 driver would have had to pay handsomely for the privilege through Mr B C Ecclestone's Formula One Administration empire. For the moment, however, the motorcycle dealer from Bexleyheath in suburban London had to content himself with tenth place in the F3 final, which was won by a youthful Stirling Moss.

Ecclestone once remarked: "I was a sort of Jean Alesi-style driver. I either won or I spun off." Most agree that this was putting a somewhat optimistic and upbeat retrospective gloss on his level of motor racing achievement. He was certainly a feisty little driver, not averse to rubbing wheels with his rivals, yet scrutiny of the F3 records in the 1950s reflects a certain paucity of hard results. His cars, however, were always immaculate. So no surprises there.

Both Ecclestone and Mosley have always known much about the global sport they now spectacularly dominate. Mosley also competed, albeit with modest results, in the admittedly highly competitive

Formula 2 series of the 1960s, and both operated F1 teams in the 1970s, during which they accumulated a very shrewd awareness of the qualities required to operate in the fast-moving F1 business.

The history of March Engineering, of which Mosley was one of the founders, set the tone for the sport's expansion in the 1970s. Max had raced in the Clubmans sports cars in the mid-1960s before graduating into international Formula 2 – the then-equivalent of Formula 3000 – as the sport's key feeder category which delivered bright young stars into the Formula 1 firmament.

That Mosley was brave behind the wheel was not in doubt. This was a man, remember, who did more than 20 parachute jumps when he was serving in the Territorial Army, Britain's reserve forces. There is a well-developed streak of audacious superiority in his character, which has matured into a formidable toughness in his role as FIA president. You do not mess with Mosley. His *modus operandi* may have a more obviously sophisticated gloss than that deployed by Ecclestone, but the same steel lurks just below the surface.

Ecclestone's commercial far-sightedness was his single most remarkable quality. He had shrewdly assessed the investment required to make F1 a serious business and calculated that its potential as a global sport was almost unmatched.

03: TAKING ON THE WORLD

By the middle of the 1970s, F1 had expanded far beyond its original European heartland. True enough, it may have seemed an audacious adventure as Bernie journeyed to Casablanca in 1958 as helper and manager of Vanwall driver Stuart Lewis-Evans. But nobody who recalls the compact, slightly anonymous figure who often accompanied Lewis-Evans could have remotely imagined what he might eventually accomplish.

Just 13 years later, when Bernie was on the point of purchasing the Brabham team, F1's popularity was steadily expanding. There were regular fixtures in South Africa and the USA, Canada and Argentina. Brazil was due to join up, and in 1976 the first race through the streets of the Californian coastal city of Long Beach further enhanced the sport's diversity.

Races outside Europe had been intermittently included on the calendar over the years. Argentina staged its first round of the World Championship as early as 1953, on the back of Juan Manuel Fangio's emergence as the country's greatest international sportsman. Fangio was in a works Maserati on that occasion, but the race's place in history was secured by a terrible accident in which Giuseppe Farina's Ferrari Tipo 500 slewed into a group of spectators who had crowded too close to the edge of the circuit. Nine were killed, 40 injured.

Truly, this was motor racing in the raw, after a fashion one could hardly imagine half a century later.

From 1950 to '59 the Indianapolis 500, the blue riband oval track race of the American racing calendar, was included as a qualifying round of the World Championship. The fact that there was almost no interchange of competitors between this event and the main body of the Formula 1 title chase seemed neither here nor there. This strange state of affairs ended after the '59 500, at the start of a season which saw the first proper US Grand Prix take place on the bumpy Sebring aerodrome circuit in Florida.

That first US race grabbed the headlines as the event in which Jack Brabham won the first of his three World Championships, and British Ferrari driver Tony Brooks lost his chance of taking the title through what amounted to personal choice, when faced with a very difficult set of circumstances.

Brooks and championship rival Brabham had endured a nerve-racking three-month wait following the Italian Grand Prix on 13 September, before the US fixture rounded off the season on 12 December. Brooks qualified as the fastest Ferrari runner, on the inside of the second row of the grid, but was rammed on the opening lap by team-mate Wolfgang von Trips's sister car. Brooks revealed his own very firm personal philosophy by making a precautionary pit stop to check for damage. It cost him his chance of the world title.

He explained simply: "Life is a gift from God, I believe, so you do not have the right to take your own life. In a war, or some set of threatening circumstances, I'm prepared to put my life on the line with the next man. But what we were engaged in was a sport.

"So I reasoned that I did not have the right to take a totally unreasonable risk with my life. What I interpreted as loading the dice against me unreasonably was driving a mechanically deficient motor car.

"I had earlier had two lessons on that subject; one was a sticking throttle in the BRM at the 1956 British GP, which resulted in it turning over and throwing me out, and the other trying to get the Aston Martin out of fourth gear and rolling at Tertre Rouge (at Le Mans), ending up trapped underneath the car.

"Both of those were stupidity errors rather than driver errors. They reminded me that motor racing was dangerous enough, and I decided that if I was ever faced with that dilemma again, I would definitely come in and get the car checked.

"At Sebring, this was a terribly difficult decision to make. It was not the biggest shunt of all time, but the point is that when you stress a component in a way it isn't designed to be stressed, relatively low impact speeds can cause a problem.

"Clearly, if I came in, I was going to have blown my Championship chance, but I felt that I would have not been true to myself if I hadn't honoured the promise I had made to myself after those previous two accidents. So I had to force myself to come in to be true to myself. The easiest thing would have been to continue, but I would have betrayed myself. One likes to live comfortably with oneself and not have regrets.

"Ferrari never castigated me in any way, but I do not think he was very pleased. I think it was completely contrary to what Ferrari expected. But I don't think he understood this sort of philosophy, perhaps many people do not. I finished third, but needed to win to take the Championship." It was his last race for the Prancing Horse.

When Michael Schumacher recklessly drove his Ferrari into the side of Jacques Villeneuve's Williams as they battled for the lead of the European Grand Prix at Jerez 38 years later, the German driver might have hailed from a different planet to that inhabited by Brooks. The difference was, of course, that the passage of four decades had made the cars and circuits unimaginably safe by the prehistoric standards of the 1950s. Which was why, of course, the sport had become engulfed in a flood tide of sloppy, undisciplined driving. But that's another story.

The 1960s saw the US Grand Prix firmly established on the World Championship schedule. It took place at California's Riverside circuit in 1960 and then moved to the Watkins Glen track, amidst the spectacular forests of upstate New York, where it remained from 1961 through to 1980.

The United States was regarded as a huge area of potential expansion for F1 during the 1960s and '70s. Californian Phil Hill had become the country's first world champion in 1961 and, although his frontline F1 career quickly faded thereafter, New York-born Dan Gurney was amongst the most competitive of all F1 performers until the end of the decade.

This was followed by the emergence of the charismatic Mario Andretti, who would become the first, and so far only, American to win a round of the World Championship on his home soil, at Long Beach in 1977.

The development of Long Beach highlighted the entrepreneurial abilities of Chris Pook, an expatriate British one-time travel agent who had ended up in California during the 1960s. Pook was a passionate motor racing enthusiast, but with an astute business brain. He had a vision that he was determined to pursue, namely changing the Californian seaside resort's image from that of a retirement town to a thriving attraction for tourists. The concept was initially mocked by the local community, but Pook persisted and formed a race committee with Dan Gurney, by then retired from F1, offering valuable advice. Politicians were lobbied in the surrounding area and ultimately the City Fathers gave the green light for the project in November 1974.

Long Beach was a pioneering race in more ways than one. Its arrival on the calendar represented the thrust of the ambitious entrepreneur over the traditionalist blue blazer brigade, if you like. More specifically, Pook managed to tap into the imagination of the paying spectator whose attention had previously been monopolised, in a motor racing context, very largely by the spectacle of NASCAR and Indycar machinery racing wheel-to-wheel on high-banked ovals. Road racing may have thrived at Watkins Glen since the early post-war, pre-F1 era, but selling the Formula 1 World Championship to a West Coast US audience was always going to be a more demanding challenge.

It also signalled that local government could be harnessed to offer support for a Formula 1 race, if it could be demonstrated that there was a benefit for the local community. Admittedly that had been going on for decades within the confines of the Principality of Monaco, but that was a special case where the economy was totally reliant on such once-a-year spectacles to keep its coffers nicely replenished. Ecclestone watched with interest as Pook – who to this day respectfully refers to him as "Bernard" rather than "Bernie", as does Sir Frank Williams – sought to finance his new project by selling stock in the Long Beach Grand Prix Corporation, of which he also became president.

Existing roads were modified and safety systems provided, including nearly five miles of concrete barriers, 25,000 old car tyres to act as energy absorbers, debris fencing, and 1500 oil drums filled with sand against which to anchor the guard rails.

As a warm-up to the first F1 Grand Prix – scheduled for 28 March 1976 – a Formula 5000 race was staged the previous September. It proved that Pook was thinking along the correct lines. It attracted 85,000 spectators, and that was followed up by 77,000 spectators attending the F1 race over three days. Despite its apparent popularity, and obvious boost to the local economy, the first race lost an estimated $281,000. Add to that the loss on the F5000 race, which included the original cost of equipping the circuit, and the total loss was around $600,000.

Nevertheless, the Long Beach City Council was anxious to run the race again in 1977 and duly deferred payments due to them. In addition, the Long Beach Convention and News Bureau, a non-profit corporation financed by local businessmen to promote the city, reportedly loaned the GP Corporation $135,000 in return for a hand in organising the 1977 event.

After this shaky start, the Long Beach GP flourished as a round of the world championship until 1983. Pook then told Ecclestone quite firmly that there was no way in which he could continue to afford the reputed $3.5m payment for staging the F1 race demanded by FOCA, the Formula One Constructors Association under whose banner Ecclestone then ran Formula 1.

Instead, on race morning that year, he confirmed that the Long Beach GP was switching to a CART fixture for 1984, something which would save $1m a year. At the time, Ecclestone brushed aside the notion that cost had anything to do with it. He claimed that Pook had fallen out with the CBS television network and, as a result, a professional television package – which many saw as vital to FOCA's existence – could not be guaranteed for the future.

Two decades later, Ecclestone would continue to repudiate the rumour that Pook had "faced him down" in the negotiations over the question of Long Beach's future as a round of the F1 World Championship. Either way, Long Beach has continued to thrive to this day as a round of the CART championship. And, word has it, Bernie is still one of the shareholders in this highly successful event.

A few years earlier, Brazil had emerged as one of the most powerful forces in F1, riding on the back of Emerson Fittipaldi's arrival on the scene as the youngest world champion of all time in 1972. Brazil, in effect, had its own Chris Pook, an imaginative and personable businessman called Antonio Scavone. "Tony", as he was known, initially masterminded the F3 and F2 series which put Brazil on the international motorsporting map between 1969 and '72.

Then, recruiting the support of the national TV Globo television network for the necessary backing, he staged a non-championship F1 race at Sao Paulo's Interlagos circuit in 1972, followed by a fully fledged championship round the following year, which was won, gratifyingly for the passionate capacity crowd, by Fittipaldi in his Lotus 72.

Scavone by now had become informally dubbed Brazil's "Mr Motor Racing", but his role was to be literally short-lived. Flying to Europe for the 1973 British Grand Prix, he was a passenger on a Varig Boeing 707 which suffered a cabin fire on the approach to Orly airport in Paris. Eventually the pilot put the crippled plane down in a field a couple of miles short of the runway, but all the passengers had been asphyxiated even before the aircraft hit the ground. Three decades after his death, Scavone is recalled with affection and regard as a popular personality and a man who left an enduring legacy to subsequent generations of Brazilian motor racing fans.

The 1980s also saw F1 plunder a variety of disparate venues across North America. It went to Las Vegas (1981-82), Detroit (1982-88), again sponsored by the City Fathers, then to Dallas for a one-off round in 1984 and to Phoenix, Arizona, for races in 1989 to 1991. Yet somehow F1 in the USA just did not generally seem to grab the fans' attention in the way that Long Beach had managed to do. When the Phoenix organisers claimed 40,000 spectators for their first qualifying session in 1989, one journalist cast his eyes at the thinly populated grandstands and remarked that "they must have come disguised as empty seats".

Or perhaps it was simply the lack of an American driver that caused the problem, Mario Andretti having driven his last Grand Prix around the car park of the Caesars Palace hotel complex in Las Vegas in 1982. Fourteen years had passed since Mario started the 1968 US Grand Prix at Watkins Glen from pole position at the wheel of a Lotus 49B, so at least there was a nice symmetry to the fact that his F1 career had been book-ended by two American races. Yet Las Vegas, again, was about as far away from the genteel, rural surroundings of New England as it was possible to get.

There was more to come. The 1985 season would see Australia join the championship schedule with a race through the streets of Adelaide. The state government of South Australia chipped in to help here, but then Ecclestone found that Melbourne, fronted by successful businessman Ron Walker, was prepared to raise the stakes in a bid to switch the race to the state capital of Victoria.

The news of the switch was greeted with a mixture of competitive delight and thinly veiled disgust in Australia. Adelaide, Australia's answer to the refined charms of Cheltenham in many people's eyes, looked as though it was being shorn of its major international sporting event. Apart from test cricket, of course. Melbourne, more cosmopolitan and brassy and once a venue for the Olympic Games back in 1956, seemed to be exerting unfair muscle on its smaller competitor.

The arrival of the F1 World Championship at Melbourne's spectacularly revamped Albert Park circuit did not attract the unreserved support of the local populace, either. A vocal minority of so-called conservationists took exception to what they regarded as the ecological vandalising of a public park, ignoring the majority consensus that this downtown area had degenerated into something of a dump in recent years, and the investment in the new circuit had considerably spruced up the whole place.

"Taxpayers slugged $80m just for a motor race," stormed one advertisement in a local newspaper. "Join the March! Sunday 10 March, 1pm." According to the dissenters, the Victorian state government had squandered more than A$55m of public money "chainsawing down more than 10,000 trees, pouring 42,000 square metres of bitumen, erecting ugly pit buildings and gouging underpasses." But it was also reported that "race fans" were stopping Bernie Ecclestone in the paddock, warmly shaking his hand and thanking him for bringing the race to their city. F1 regulars smiled quietly. A run-of-the-mill "race fan" had about as much chance of gaining access to the F1 paddock as he had of getting into Fort Knox.

After Australia, where next? The answer was Malaysia in 1999. Another track bankrolled by the government for reasons of national prestige, an event which did not have to make a profit. Nor did it, at least for the first couple of years. This was all in line with Max and Bernie's professed belief that F1 should be a more representative "world championship" than the Europe-biased contest it had been in the past.

Such apparently balanced, visionary thinking may have concealed a secondary agenda. The teams and the FIA were preparing for a head-on clash with the European Union and threatening to take many of the races away from a geographic area where anti-tobacco legislation was increasingly impinging on the teams' ability to raise massive operating budgets.

In 2000, Ecclestone managed to pull off the coup of coups, not only returning F1 to the USA, but taking it directly into the heartland of American motorsport with a US Grand Prix at Indianapolis. In doing so, Bernie concluded a deal with the Hulman-George family, owners of the Indianapolis Motor Speedway, who are the closest thing to royalty that they have in this otherwise unremarkable midwestern industrial city.

When the starting lights finally went out to mark the start of the first F1 race at the famous "Brickyard", it marked another dramatic milestone in the history of this unique American icon – and the dynasty which had steered the fortunes of the most famous race track in America for more than 55 years.

The man in charge is Anton Hulman "Tony" George, the 41-year -old president and chief executive of the Indianapolis Motor Speedway Corporation, home since 1911 to what is claimed to be the largest single-day sporting event in the world, the Indianapolis 500. Yet it would be easy to say that George decided to cut a deal with Ecclestone to bring the US Grand Prix to Indianapolis in order to bolster the circuit's fading image.

In 1995 George precipitated a split with the US CART series to establish the Indy Racing League "to preserve the traditions and excitement of America's open-wheel oval track racing". Subsequently, the Indy 500 survived more off the back of its legendary reputation than the star quality of its competitors. By 2000, however, the trend showed signs of being reversed as future Williams F1 driver Juan Pablo Montoya paid his first visit to the speedway and won easily.

By then Tony George was well down the road to completing the reputed $72m expenditure necessary to upgrade Indianapolis with a state-of-the-art grand prix circuit which, cleverly, incorporates part of the banked track which has made Indianapolis so famous.

However George, who represents the Hulman family's third generation ownership of the circuit, continued the family's reputation for shrewd business acumen. For the first F1 race the fans paid just $32 for basic admission rather than the equivalent of $144 that British fans had to spend at the same year's rain-spoiled British GP at Silverstone.

"We want to give the fans good value," said George. "If we had priced the tickets at the sort of levels seen at some European races, we would have been disappointed to have got only 30,000 to 40,000 spectators." As it was, the race was a sell-out with some 209,000 tickets sold.

"We intend to further broaden the fan base," George continued. "Part of the problem for Formula 1 in the USA has been lack of stability; the race did not have the chance to stabilise itself for a period of time at one venue. But we believe we have sufficient resources to reinforce in the public mind what they can expect from the race."

Gradually the fans seem to be taking to the F1 business, although the stupidity of the Ferrari drivers in attempting to enact a wheel-to-wheel finish between Michael Schumacher and Rubens Barrichello at the end of the 2002 race attracted huge criticism from the local media, which pointed out that American fans are not used to staged events. This remark prompted a wry smile from those who believe that NASCAR is not averse to spicing up its racing by what might loosely be termed "artificial means", but certainly the Ferrari approach was heavy-handed and unsubtle.

It was on 14 November 1945, that Tony George's grandfather,

Tony Hulman, a businessman from Terre Haute, Indiana, had obtained control of the down-at-heel Indianapolis Motor Speedway. He purchased the crumbling, careworn track from Captain Eddie Rickenbacker, the legendary First World War flying ace, for $750,000. It was a shrewd deal. Rickenbacker and his associates had originally purchased the speedway for the same sum in 1927 and, on the face of it, came out of the deal with no profit.

Yet in the uncertain economic climate in the months after the end of the Second World War, Rickenbacker must have been happy to escape with his shirt. Over the decades since then, Indianapolis has been home to a very specialised form of motor racing. European *aficionados* used to pour scorn on the huge 1950s front-engined roadsters, running on truck tyres, and their brawny drivers whose only task was to turn left four times a lap.

Yet in 1957, when the Indy roadsters crossed the Atlantic for a challenge race against the best Europe could provide, the F1 teams boycotted the race on the grounds that the Italian combined road and banked circuit at Monza was excessively dangerous.

Unabashed, the legendary Indycar tough guy Jimmy Bryan went out and lapped Monza at an average speed of 176mph, unlit cigar clamped firmly between his teeth, before returning to the pits nonchalantly brushing his shoulder.

"That ain't hayseed," he growled. "It's dandruff."

Bryan won the 1958 Indianapolis 500 but was killed racing two years later.

Quite what he – and indeed Tony George's grandfather – would have made of a United States Grand Prix at Indianapolis can only be left to the imagination. Selling out to the enemy, perhaps?

04: DOLLARS TO DIE FOR; F1'S FIRST MILLIONAIRE

Whilst Ecclestone crafted the future of the sport's commercial development, he was far from its first millionaire. That distinction fell to Jackie Stewart, the dyslexic Scottish lad from Dumbarton who started out cleaning the lubrication bay at his father's local garage. Within ten years he had become the sport's first dollar millionaire, shrewdly managed by Mark McCormack's IMG organisation, the agency which made Arnold Palmer and other top golfers household names across the world.

It may seem small beer today, but when Stewart was paid 20,000 pounds by Ken Tyrrell in 1968, the motor racing world rocked on its heels. He was the world's top-earning driver, at a time when a middle-ranking provincial British bank manager could count himself lucky to earn 2200 pounds. That meant that Stewart was earning nine times an ordinary, day-to-day salary earned by a middle-class, mid-income bracket, family man.

Today Michael Schumacher, the best driver in the world, is estimated to earn around 22m pounds for his talents behind the wheel.

Yet there are clearly no provincial British bank managers earning more than 2m pounds in 2003 – 60,000 pounds would be a more representative figure – and close to the top of the scale, at that. Cost inflation at the top end of the F1 market for drivers has accelerated off the scale. And it has all been fuelled by F1's success as a televised spectacular.

During Stewart's F1 heyday, there were more pressing priorities than simply earning big money. The big challenge was to live long enough to enjoy it.

Jackie made his Grand Prix debut in the 1965 South African GP at East London, driving a BRM V8. He had completed 99 World Championship qualifying races by the time he hung up his helmet just over eight years later. He had been three times world champion, won a then-record 27 Grands Prix. And seen no fewer than eight of his colleagues killed in action in those races, as well as experiencing the death of the legendary Jim Clark, a fellow Scot and soulmate, in an F2 race at Hockenheim – the race in which Max Mosley made his F2 debut in that Brabham BT23C.

Today Stewart is Sir Jackie, long-retired, a multi-millionaire, the president of the British Racing Drivers' Club and a man who moves easily in the company of royalty and political figures.

At Monaco in 1997, his fledgling Stewart-Ford team had its transporter positioned well away from the main paddock area. On the face of it, this was because his team were newcomers.

"Since he knows Prince Rainier so well, we thought he might like to have his team a bit nearer to the palace," said one of Ecclestone's minions in a mocking tone. Jackie affected to be unabashed, but F1 insiders report that he has faced Ecclestone and Mosley down on at least one highly political occasion relating to the sport's drawn-out problems with the European Union. Jackie is not a man to be lightly dismissed.

Those with an uncharitable bent poke fun at Stewart. They mock his squeaky voice, his penchant for name-dropping. Yet he is absolutely beyond reproach, a man who has no skeletons in his cupboard. He is also a man who has – on several occasions – been pitched, directly or indirectly, into head-to-heads with Mosley and Ecclestone. For one thing, he maintained an unyielding anti-tobacco sponsorship stance when he set up the Stewart-Ford team with his son Paul at the start of the 1997 F1 season. And he refused to modify it to help the FIA's stance against the EU anti-tobacco legislation.

It was all a far cry from May 1974, when Jackie and his wife Helen set off from Glasgow to drive to Monaco in an MGB sports car. They stopped to stay with F1 driver Bruce McLaren in Surbiton, an outer London suburb. When they got to Dover, they found that their ferry tickets and travellers cheques had blown off the roof of the car back in rural Surrey as they accelerated away on their journey.

Consequently they had to invest in a pair of one-way air tickets to the Mediterranean principality. Thankfully, they got there with plenty of time for Jackie to win the prestigious Monaco Grand Prix F3 supporting race, a success which launched the 25-year-old Scot on the road to fame, fortune and three World Championship crowns.

"We were staying in Rocquebrune, just along the coast, and on the first day we walked into Monaco because I did not have enough money for a taxi," he said. "But I won the F3 race, which attracted more prize money than third place in the Grand Prix. At the gala dinner I sat alongside Princess Grace – and then drove back to England in a borrowed Ford Zodiac towing an empty trailer."

The Stewarts never had to walk to Monaco again. From then on, Jackie and Helen would regularly dine at Monaco's royal palace as personal guests of Prince Rainier. He won the fairy-tale race on no fewer than three occasions – 1966, '71 and '73.

More than any other driver of the post-war era, Jackie Stewart is synonymous with Monaco. Graham Hill, Ayrton Senna, Alain Prost and Michael Schumacher may have won more races there, but the length of Stewart's association is unparalleled in Formula 1 history. By 1997 his own team, Stewart Grand Prix, contested the Monaco

Grand Prix for the first time and Rubens Barrichello finished a magnificent second behind Michael Schumacher's Ferrari.

"I said at the time that I got more satisfaction from our team finishing second here than I ever did from winning the race myself," Stewart recalled. "That was a superb performance which owed very little to luck".

Thirty years earlier, he had watched in horror from the pits as Lorenzo Bandini's Ferrari crashed at the waterfront chicane and exploded in a fireball which left the popular Italian mortally injured. The tragedy strengthened Stewart's determination to crusade for improved motor racing safety, a task which brought him into head-on collision with the sport's traditionalists.

"It was another example of the incredibly poor facilities which existed in motor racing at that time," he said. "It was a big fire, another demonstration of how inadequate the whole business was in terms of safety. You found yourself becoming an expert at finding those undertakers with the necessary expertise to move bodies from country to country, you found out that some airlines would not carry a coffin in a passenger plane.

"Monaco was always a daunting circuit. In the 1960s the kerbs were straight-cut – not chamfered (sloped), as they are today – and there were lamp posts at the side of the track all the way up the hill. By today's standards it was primitive. Yet I still find the whole place gives me an unbelievable buzz. The skyline has always been wonderful, the whole setting unbelievable."

By general consent, Stewart scored one of the very best wins of his career at Monaco in 1971. Despite suffering from a badly upset stomach, he qualified his Tyrrell-Ford on pole position, only to find the brake balance bar broken as he took his place on the grid, leaving him with braking on the front wheels only. Unconcerned, he led from start to finish, then was sick on the winner's rostrum.

With a touch of false modesty he plays down the magnitude of that achievement. "Although you might not think so, Monaco is not particularly hard on brakes because you are never slowing from really high speed," he said. "But it was a good race. To do it with only two-wheel braking was quite something. It's also worth remembering that we had manual gearboxes in those days – and that meant a maximum of 2800 gearchanges during the course of the race with the six-speed box we had on the old BRM. You always ended the race with your gearchange hand badly blistered."

Stewart resolutely stood out for safety improvements at a time when he was regarded as an eccentric by the dyed-in-the-wool traditionalists who believed that the risk of death or serious injury was all part and parcel of the challenge. How, asked the detractors, could it be worthwhile if there was no danger involved? Surely cheating death was part of the attraction?

No, responded Stewart. Not so. I'm paid to drive and demonstrate my skill. Not to kill myself.

His most ardent critic was the late Denis Jenkinson, continental correspondent of the respected British magazine *Motor Sport*. Jenkinson at least spoke from a position of strength. A sparky, sometimes spikey dwarf of a man, he had sat alongside Eric Oliver to win the 1949 World Sidecar Championship, and then sat alongside Stirling Moss to win the 1955 Mille Miglia road race around Italy in a Mercedes-Benz 300SLR.

After one particularly vitriolic outburst from Jenkinson, Stewart wrote to *Motor Sport* from his Swiss office at Gland, near Geneva, to set the record straight. He respected Jenkinson, but remained baffled in his own mind as to how an apparently intelligent observer could be so backward in his thinking.

"I try terribly hard, devoting considerable time and effort to make motor racing as a whole, for as many people as possible – officials, spectators, drivers and even journalists – safer than it has been in the past," he wrote to the magazine on 13 June 1972.

"The sport will never be totally safe, and I perhaps know that better than Mr Jenkinson could ever know. But it is imperative that people act in a positive and constructive way to bring race-track safety, medical and fire-fighting facilities up to modern standards.

"It is very easy to sit on the fence and criticise – notoriously easy. You can always find faults in what the other people are doing, but at least they are doing something. All Mr Jenkinson seems to do is lament the drivers who have served their time in it. Few of them however are alive to read his writings.

"If a present-day driver criticises a new modern racing facility, he is often applauded by the Jenkinsons of this world as being made of 'good old stuff,' but if he condemns one of the old-established race tracks for lack of proper facilities, he is shot at by the same people and accused of trying to damage the sport or even of being cowardly."

Later in the narrative Stewart adds: "What Denis Jenkinson thinks or says concerns me little. To me he is a fence sitter, doing little or nothing to secure a future for our sport. The readers of *Motor Sport*, however, are much more important. I would like to say to them that whatever criticism I get will make no difference at all to my personal effort to make motor racing, of all classes, safer for as many people as possible within our sport.

"There is nothing more tragically sad than mourning a man who has died under circumstances which could have been avoided had someone done something beforehand. It therefore always angers me to hear of people who oppose an effort to make our sport safer and therefore reduce the tragic losses that we have all painfully experienced.

"Such men to me are hypocrites, the only consolation being that in years to come they will probably be looked back on as cranks."

There was a delightful sequel to all this some 15 years later when we attended the Detroit Grand Prix and Stewart arranged for a group of us, including Jenkinson, to pay a visit to Ford's road car test track, close to the company's headquarters in nearby Dearborn. The two of them were immersed in deep conversation for much of the drive back into Detroit, after which Jenkinson remarked to me casually: "Good bloke, old Stewart."

When Jenks died on 29 November 1996, many of the F1 fraternity were waiting to see whether his funeral would clash with the official unveiling of the new Stewart-Ford Grand Prix challenger. It did not, as things turned out, but Jenks would have been amused if he had taken a last shot at his old rival from beyond the grave.

It said much for Stewart's innate good nature that he indulged Jenkinson's barbs with as much patience as he did. Basically, he respected his right to an opinion, even though he believed he was crackers.

"Jenks's passing truly marks the end of an era," said Stewart. "He was a genuine eccentric, yet he never *knew* that he was an eccentric. Many enjoy the image of eccentricity, but Jenks was the genuine article.

"His views were always from his heart – and I got more venom than most from him at the time. But I admired him as a journalist and I like to think he admired me, to some extent, as a driver. He was someone very special and we should all be grateful to have known him."

Stewart for many years was active and campaigning in his role as president of the Grand Prix Drivers' Association (GPDA). He knew that the drivers were the key to the sport's success. Ultimately, strong though the Formula One Constructors Association (FOCA) would become during the 1970s, Jackie appreciated that it was a *World Drivers'* Championship, first and foremost.

The fans came to see the *drivers*, not – with the exception of Ferrari – the cars. This was a viewpoint not everybody shared, yet Ecclestone was shrewd enough to take the implicit point. The drivers may have been the stars, but to build a cohesive powerbase on which to exploit the sport's commercial potential would mean getting all the teams together under a single umbrella. This was not like golf, where the presence of a key star player could make or break a tournament. If one could control the teams, then the drivers' loyalty would inevitably follow. In the wake of Stewart, and his equally firmly safety-oriented successors Emerson Fittipaldi and Niki Lauda, the drivers would eventually find they were losing their influence in mainstream F1 politics.

Stewart's drive for enhanced circuit safety had cost Spa-Francorchamps the Belgian Grand Prix and had also been responsible for upgrading the epic 14-mile Nurburgring. There was a testy confrontation over the crumbling track surface at Zolder, venue for the 1973 Belgian Grand Prix, but the crunch came at the 1975 Spanish Grand Prix. A pre-race inspection by GPDA representative Jean-Pierre Beltoise, then a BRM F1 driver, revealed that the guard rails on the spectacular Montjuich Park circuit had either not been installed at all – or been erected in a slipshod fashion.

Following a drivers' meeting, the GPDA decided – almost to a man – that they simply could not take part. Not a year had passed since Austrian driver Helmuth Koinigg had been decapitated in the US Grand Prix at Watkins Glen after his Surtees-Ford slid beneath an inadequately secured guard rail. In 1974, Peter Revson had also been killed at Kyalami when a technical breakage on his Shadow DN5 had sent him into an inadequately secured barrier. And it was only 18 months since Francois Cevert – Stewart's team-mate and anointed successor in the Tyrrell team – had been cut to pieces, along with his car, on a barrier at Watkins Glen.

Ronnie Peterson, who would die in 1978 when his Lotus 78 hit a barrier at Monza, emphasised that Koinigg's death meant that they could not compromise. "Before Watkins Glen last time, we all knew the guard rail was not right, because of François's accident (the previous year)," he said. "We discussed it, but we decided to go ahead and race anyway, and Helmuth was killed. Now we want to make a stand."

In the end, the race took place and only Fittipaldi, the reigning world champion, declined to take part. When Rolf Stommelen's Hill-Cosworth, leading the race, vaulted a barrier into a trackside enclosure, four onlookers were killed. The accident was caused by the failure of the car's rear wing support, and had nothing to do with the barrier. Prior to the race, Jackie Stewart had warned that if a car went into the crowd, that would possibly be the end of motor racing in Europe.

As it happened, the car did not quite go into the crowd, as such. The hapless victims had infiltrated a prohibited trackside era. F1 got away from this crisis by the skin of its teeth.

A year later, when reigning world champion Niki Lauda was burned to within an inch of his life after crashing in the German Grand Prix at Nurburgring, time was called on the epic 14-mile circuit in the Eiffel mountains. It was decided that the track was simply too dangerous and marshalling it effectively and suitably promptly was all but impossible.

This was another epic track sacrificed in the interests of safety – and the barrage of criticism which had been focused on Stewart during his campaign to reduce injury and loss of life was now directed towards Lauda. Not that Niki had anything to apologise for. Lauda's recovery from his life-threatening injuries was the stuff of which sporting legends are made.

Just over six weeks after the accident, he returned to the cockpit of a Formula 1 Ferrari for a test at Fiorano. Frankly, he was scared stiff, as he later freely admitted, but he controlled and subjugated that apprehension, to race again in the upcoming Italian GP at Monza. Despite battling a badly upset stomach, Niki qualified splendidly as the fastest of the three Ferrari competitors, lining up fifth on the inside of the third row. Come the race, Lauda twice set fastest lap in the closing stages of the Grand Prix, a time eventually bettered only by winner Ronnie Peterson's March 761. He finished fourth. He was totally drained, yet already hailed as a hero.

Lauda very nearly retained his championship. But in the rain-soaked Japanese Grand Prix at Mount Fuji, his nerve failed him and he pulled in to retire. James Hunt in a McLaren won the title by a single point. Enzo Ferrari went into a state of panic. An emotionally stunted personality at the best of times, he lacked the capacity to relate to or communicate with his drivers on anything other than a professional employer/employee relationship. His nerve endings perhaps anaesthetised by the number of drivers who had been killed and injured in his cars over the previous 25 years, he was unable to connect sympathetically with Lauda.

Things would never be the same again between the two men. Stewart, interestingly, never drove for Ferrari. The Old Man, so 'tis said, did not like the Scot's preoccupation with money. But it might have been a lucky escape. Jackie instinctively went for Tyrrell instead, winning three World Championships before Lauda won his first for Maranello in 1975, ending an 11-year drought for the Italian team.

The Grand Prix Drivers' Association had been established originally in 1961 to replace the UPPI (Union of International Professional Racing Drivers), which failed because it could not present a united front. The GPDA would eventually follow suit and from the 1977 South African Grand Prix, the GPDA effectively fell into Ecclestone's orbit as a component of FOCA. But this would be a temporary eclipse; by the start of the 1982 season the drivers would again be at loggerheads with FOCA at the South African GP.

Reflecting on his own career, Stewart said: "On the commercial side, I'm glad I saw the opportunities I did and pleased that some of the things I did rubbed off and, of course, the sport has become a commercial giant since I retired in 1973.

"But I feel that I have been part of that movement, all of which has been very positive and beneficial for the sport as a whole. My regret is that most of the drivers have not appreciated with the same foresight the benefits that can be realised and have allowed themselves, somehow or another, almost to be overshadowed by the sport rather than remaining in the spotlight, centre stage."

Then, in what could be interpreted as an oblique swipe at Ecclestone, he added: "The Formula One Constructors' Association was created almost in the fear that the drivers would continue to have the prominence and power that I was enjoying at the pinnacle of my career.

"I think that was very threatening to a lot of people in the business who felt this situation should never be permitted to develop again. But the drivers (by 1991) have allowed themselves to be suffocated far too much and they do not have the power and position in the sport that they should have.

"It was my experience when I was the president of the Grand Prix Drivers' Association that the drivers themselves are sadly lethargic about even those matters which would be to their benefit, and even more lethargic towards anything benefiting fellow competitors.

"They have somehow allowed themselves to become bypassed, used and sometimes abused in a fashion which I find very distasteful. But, on the other hand, if people are prepared to be walked on, then they will be used as carpets. It is their own doing. No one seems to be prepared to stand up and put in the work necessary to earn that position of authority and power.

"At the end of the day, however big may be the names of the teams, it is the drivers who sit in those cars and provide the human element, the focal point of public interest."

In 1997 Stewart appeared back on the F1 pit wall, overseeing the fortunes of Stewart Grand Prix, his much-publicised new F1 team, which would carry the fortunes of Ford when it replaced Sauber as the global car giant's front line F1 representative. For three seasons, the Stewart-Fords raced as respectable mid-grid cars, their great day coming in the 1999 European Grand Prix at the new Nurburgring where Johnny Herbert gave the team its maiden, and only, F1 win. By then the team had been sold to Ford for about $80m, as Detroit prepared to re-brand the outfit under the Jaguar name.

Since then, it has hardly been an unqualified success. Stewart is still an influential voice on the F1 scene, even though he does not come to all the races. Yet his opinions are still valued, listened to by some with polite respect, ignored by others who feel that he has enjoyed his place in the F1 sun for too long, and perhaps now might give consideration to piping down.

Yet most of his views make perfect sense. In particular, he has felt that F1 driver discipline had not been given sufficient attention over the years. In his view it all began to go wrong in 1970 when Clay Regazzoni shamelessly weaved around on the straight at Monza to break the slipstream between him and Stewart's pursuing March. Although this was an accepted driving technique to an extent at the time, Stewart felt it represented the start of a breakdown in overall driver discipline which continues to this day.

Jackie also fell foul of Regazzoni when the Ferrari driver elbowed his Tyrrell-Ford into the scenery at the old Nurburgring during the 1972 German Grand Prix. Regazzoni's Ferrari continued, to finish the race second behind team-mate Jacky Ickx, but Stewart – ironically protected from possible injury by the guard rails he had championed – was left with a long walk home.

He may be only a few years away from drawing his state pension, but Jackie is still sharp enough to detect a direct line between what Regazzoni did 30 years ago and the stunt Schumacher pulled on Villeneuve at Jerez in 1997 as they battled for the World Championship in the European Grand Prix. And he certainly does not mince his words.

"It seemed to most people so obvious that (Michael) had a choice and he chose to drive in that direction," he said, "particularly when there was a lot of race track still there, because by then Villeneuve was on a piece of track which he probably did not want to be on. It would have been very easy for Michael to have moved over and avoided the collision.

"It was also very fortunate that there was no interlocking of wheels. It could have ended in tears; as it was it ended in embarrassment, to some extent for the whole racing fraternity."

Stewart believed there was also a secondary reason why this sort of behaviour should be stepped on. When young kids in karts and Formula Ford see Michael Schumacher getting away with such behaviour, it becomes legitimised in their minds. In other words, do not store up grief for the Silverstone Club race stewards by failing to take a firm line with multiple world champions.

One problem Jackie faces is akin to that which he encountered while banging the safety drum back in the late 1960s. People got bored with the message. Yet that in no way invalidates his argument. He believes that one day the nightmare scenario will occur.

Remember Christian Fittipaldi's backward roll over Minardi team-mate Pierluigi Martini across the finish line at Monza in 1993?

And Riccardo Patrese's Williams almost hitting the bridge over the track at Estoril after rearing up over Gerhard Berger's innocently slowing McLaren?

Such elements will, sooner or later, conspire again to cause a tragic multiple accident. "So this sort of behaviour does not just have to be discouraged," said Stewart. "It has to be eliminated." In a word, no more namby-pamby turning a blind eye, as the FIA stewards did when Ayrton Senna's McLaren rammed Alain Prost's Ferrari off the road at Suzuka nine seconds after the start of the 1990 Japanese Grand Prix.

When Schumacher tried to turf Villeneuve off the track at Jerez in 1997, the FIA loftily announced that he would be deprived of his points for that season. "It is a very severe penalty being deprived of a vice-championship," said FIA president Max Mosley with suitable gravitas.

Had I not been present at the press conference where he uttered those words, I wouldn't have credited it. "Excuse me, is it April Fool's Day?", I muttered to a colleague. A fellow scribe asked Mosley whether Schumacher would have had his points totally wiped out if he had won the championship in these same circumstances.

"Absolutely," said the FIA president. You had to admire his crust. But nobody believed him for a moment.

05: HANDLE WITH CARE; LITTLE BIG MAN

Ecclestone. Powerful, well connected, rich beyond one's wildest dreams, intimidating yet friendly in a knockabout fashion to those he knows well. A man who keeps you guessing. A good friend and a very bad enemy indeed. He once famously remarked about how to progress in business: "First you get on, then you get rich, then you get honest."

For more than a generation he has ruled the F1 infrastructure with a rod of iron.

So where did all this start? Bernie was born in 1930, the son of a trawler captain from Suffolk. His interest in motor racing stretched back to the immediate post-war years when he raced a motorcycle on the grass track at Brands Hatch when he was only a teenager.

Distinguished motorcycle champion John Surtees recalls being taken by his father to buy motorcycle parts from Bernie's family home in the early post-war years, the future Brabham boss apparently operating out of his mother's kitchen at the time. Although Bernie actually studied chemistry, albeit briefly, at Woolwich Polytechnic, his true talents proved to be as a dealer. The world of commerce was destined to take him a long way from his modest beginnings.

He first raced in 500cc F3 back in the 1950s, and became an active and enthusiastic car racer, first at the wheel of a Formula 3 Cooper, later with a Cooper-Bristol single-seater and a Cooper-Jaguar sports car. In 1958 he made an unsuccessful attempt to qualify a Connaught – one of two that he had purchased at the auction of assets when the British F1 team closed its doors the previous year – for the Monaco Grand Prix, by which time he was managing the interests of British driver Stuart Lewis-Evans, who was driving in the Vanwall team alongside Stirling Moss and Tony Brooks.

Sadly, Lewis-Evans suffered what were to prove fatal burns when he crashed in the 1958 Moroccan Grand Prix, and Bernie dropped from the racing scene to concentrate on his business interests. When he reappeared on the scene eight years later, it was as business manager of Jochen Rindt. The Austrian was killed at Monza practising for the 1970 Italian Grand Prix at the wheel of a Lotus 72.

Bernie was a close friend of Rindt, and the godfather of his daughter Natascha, now 35, who worked for several years with FOCA TV as a producer before making a career as a pilot. Her father's death touched Ecclestone deeply. Bernie had been partnered with him in Jochen Rindt Racing, the semi-works Lotus Formula 2 team, and continued running those cars briefly through the winter of 1970/71. Natascha would later fly one of Bernie's private jets for him, a reflection of his loyalty to true friends which would again surface in his friendship with Ayrton Senna, the legendary Brazilian driver who was killed in the 1994 San Marino Grand Prix.

However, Bernie, who had made a success of the motorcycle and car sales business as well as some shrewd and timely property dealings, by now had bigger ambitions. It was even suggested, unwisely as I recall, that Ecclestone was involved in the 1963 Great Train Robbery which netted around 2.6m pounds – worth some 40m pounds at today's values. When this suggestion was aired in a national newspaper, Bernie sued and rightly obtained a retraction.

Bernie was certainly well acquainted with Roy James, nick-named "The Weasel", who was given a 30-year prison sentence for his part in the heist as one of the getaway drivers. This was hardly surprising, of course, since everybody in the motor racing fraternity knew James as one of the brightest young Formula Junior racers of the early 1960s.

As an aside, it was reported years later that former world champion Jack Brabham – from whom James purchased his own F3 car – was called as a character witness at the trial. Asked to address the jury, Brabham glanced at the well-dressed group in the dock, turned to the judge and said wryly: "Which ones are the jury?"

When not robbing mail trains, Roy James was an accomplished silversmith. When he was released from jail in 1975 after serving just over ten years, Ecclestone commissioned him to make a silver trophy which was presented by members of the Formula One Constructors' Association to the Grand Prix they voted the best organised of the season.

In the 1950s and early 1960s, Bernie ran a motorcycle dealer-ship, Compton & Ecclestone Ltd, at 300 Broadway, Bexleyheath, Kent. At a time when most such establishments were grimy and oil-stained, Ecclestone's premises were like a new pin, the bikes all laid out in meticulously neat ranks.

The author first met Ecclestone in the spring of 1972. I was a junior reporter on the weekly motor racing paper *Motoring News* and was instructed to go down to Bernie's car dealership, James Spencer Ltd, also in Bexleyheath, to interview him in the wake of his purchase of the Brabham F1 team from its co-founder Ron Tauranac.

The episode has stuck in my mind for more than a generation. I was met by a dapper, compact man with a Beatles haircut and ush-ered up the stairs into his office, where I sat in a low chair as he perched on the desk, slightly looking down on me. This may have been intended to be slightly intimidating, but I recall he was certainly nothing but charm itself. And very amusing company.

Later he drove me in his Audi saloon to a local pub for a sandwich lunch and I was struck by the fact that every single person in the saloon bar nodded or waved in recognition: "Hi, Bernie. Alright, Bernie?" That sort of thing. We then returned to James Spencer's premises where he excused himself for a moment as a couple of potential customers came in off the street. I was then treated to a display of his persuasiveness.

While I meandered round this immaculately presented car showroom, with its E-type Jaguars standing over oil drip trays, their tyre sidewalls beautifully blackened and their used-car warranties shaped in the form of a tax disc in the licence holder on their windscreens, the middle-aged couple were ushered into a glass-faced office, which seemed to be sound-proofed. Either that, or I'd got better manners in those days and just did not try to listen.

The upshot of all this was that Bernie gave them his patter and they came out the new owners of a second-hand Humber Hawk. As I recall at the time, they'd come in to express interest in a Ford Cortina. I remember thinking that anybody who could sell a Humber Hawk under any circumstances in 1972 was, shall we say, extremely persuasive.

In fact, Ecclestone had shown a degree of interest in becoming involved in an F1 team even before the Brabham opportunity arose. Early in the 1969 season, Max Mosley decided that he would retire from race driving before he killed himself. His Lotus 59 F2 car had spun off into the bushes whilst he was practising for the Eifelrennen at the old 14-mile Nurburgring.

The accident had been caused by a suspension failure and Max took it as a warning. He was not going to make the big-time, so he decided to call time on his aspirations while he was still in one piece. Instead, he concentrated his efforts in laying the foundations of March Engineering, the ambitious new racing car constructors which he founded in partnership with former racer Alan Rees, a good mate of Rindt, designer Robin Herd and engineer Graham Coaker.

Rindt was regarded as the fastest and most spectacular F1 driver in the world at that time – a rare match for the less impulsive, more controlled Jackie Stewart. By the time Jochen left the Cooper team to join Brabham at the end of 1967, Ecclestone was managing his friend's career.

They used to fly to European races together in a jointly owned Piper Comanche – which earned the nickname of RindtStone Airways – and spent a lot of their social time together. Bernie realised that Rindt had a great personal affection for Jack Brabham, but after a dismally disappointing season wrestling with the unreliable four-cam Repco type 860 V8-engined Brabham BT24, it was clear that he was never going to win a World Championship driving for the Australian's team and he switched to Lotus for 1969.

Despite this, the personal bond between Jochen and Jack Brabham was hugely powerful. Bernie recognised this, but also appreciated that Lotus boss Colin Chapman would bid the earth to retain Jochen's services in 1970. Brabham made one last bid, backed by the Goodyear tyre company. Goodyear would fund a Brabham-Cosworth team for Rindt in 1970. But it did not come off.

Rindt and Ecclestone also tempted Robin Herd with an F1 project of his own, as the former Cosworth engineer was poised to become a co-founder of March. Robin recalls being entertained to dinner at a plush restaurant in London's West End where Bernie proposed – on Rindt's behalf – that they should establish a new team. Robin and Jochen would be 45 per cent shareholders with Bernie holding the remaining 10 per cent. It came to nothing.

Meanwhile, Max Mosley jumped into his Lotus Elan and drove down to Switzerland during the summer of '69, to the Austrian driver's home on Lake Geneva, to continue negotiations with Jochen to join March.

"But I do not believe he was ever really serious about joining March," said Max years later. "I think he just needed to convince himself that going with Robin was the right idea. He explained to me why he thought March would never get off the ground and I explained why I knew it would – and why his project would not. I liked Jochen a lot and had got to know him well when we were all racing F2 together in '68. He was stupendously quick, a phenomenon."

After Rindt was killed, Ecclestone helped wind up all the loose ends in the wake of the disaster.

By the time I first met Bernie in 1972, his foot was on the bottom step of a ladder which would eventually carry him to billionaire status.

"Ron Tauranac had initially spoken to me as early as the 1971 Monaco Grand Prix about the prospect of getting involved with him in the Brabham team," he said, "but negotiations were not completed until later that year. Ron initially asked me if I could give him some help on the business side, but later he said: 'I think I want to sell, do you want to buy half?'

"I told him that I did not particularly want to buy half, but if he wanted to sell, then I would be prepared to buy the whole business." Which is what he eventually did.

The original idea was that Tauranac should stay on in a consultancy role, but Bernie found that it just did not work out. "Ultimately, you couldn't really employ anybody who had once owned the company," he reflected. "It was not good for him and it was not good for me."

Ecclestone paid around 100,000 pounds for the Brabham team, including two completed F1 cars – a BT33 and a BT34 – and also inherited a young South African designer called Gordon Murray, one of the company's most outstanding assets, as things transpired. One of the few original thinkers in the motor racing business, Murray would design a succession of technically innovative and highly competitive Brabham F1 cars for Ecclestone for the remainder of the 1970s and much of the 1980s.

In his new role as team owner, Ecclestone would soon emerge as a leading light in the Formula One Constructors' Association. He made the time and had the mental agility necessary for this particularly specialised challenge. During the formative years of FOCA, when Bernie was negotiating TV coverage contracts and helping to bale out financially strapped race promoters, he asked the teams whether they wanted to come in with him and share the risks.

In the short-term they declined, preferring to concentrate simply on running their teams and believing that they would have an advantage if Bernie had to split his attention between Brabham and developing the F1 business, while they could concentrate on trying to beat him on the track. Perhaps they should have paid more attention to the new Brabham logo, designed by Ecclestone. It was a rearing cobra, nicknamed Hissing Sid.

Indirectly, that reluctance to share the early commercial risk of the F1 business in the 1970s and '80s contributed to the eventual imbalance of income under the Concorde Agreement and the bad feeling over Bernie's slice of the resultant financial cake.

For his part, Mosley was team principal of the STP March F1 squad from the start of the 1970 season and therefore also in on the ground floor at the start of FOCA. He and Ecclestone quickly gravitated to each other's company at those early constructors' meetings, each perhaps identifying with the other.

Both men had astonishing intellects with the capacity for instant lateral thinking. But Ecclestone was a dealer; it used to be said by his rivals in the motor trade that he could value a showroom of used cars almost at a glance. Mosley most certainly was not a wheeler-dealer – as the history of March Engineering perhaps proved – but he knew a good ally when he saw one. And Bernie would turn out to be just that.

Ecclestone also took the financial risk involved in staging some of the more commercially precarious races in the late 1970s. The other teams were not interested in taking those risks, so Bernie willingly gambled. And took any profit that was going.

Meanwhile, the Brabham team was thriving under Ecclestone's

control. By 1973 Gordon Murray was in firm charge on the technical side and developed the BT44 and BT44B generation of "pyramid monocoque" F1 cars which would win races over two seasons in the hands of Carlos Reutemann and Carlos Pace.

Bernie could be a difficult employer, insisting that the race shop at the Brabham factory should be kept as tidy as possible. Sometimes he would pick up a broom and do a bit of sweeping himself, but more often somebody would be in deep trouble if they did not get the job done to his high standards.

It was widely recounted that when ending work in the early hours, his staff did not clean up the workshop, he lined them all up the next day and said: "If I ever see this place in this state again, I'll close the team down."

He used to drive his employees crazy if a sticker was slightly out of line on a Brabham rear wing endplate. And on one legendary occasion, he is alleged to have ripped a phone off the wall after finding that its receiver had been replaced the wrong way round. "Delegation," he once remarked, "is the art of accepting second best."

He would not change his ideas as his empire burgeoned. In later years he controlled the smallest details of the worldwide business of F1, running it with an astonishingly small staff.

By the same token, Bernie was shrewd enough to realise that Murray was an unusually talented designer, and he was always prepared to allow Murray to spend money to make the Brabham cars go faster. In that respect, Bernie was extremely pragmatic; the better the cars went, the more success they would achieve and the richer he would become on the back of that success.

Today's F1 television coverage has achieved global levels of exposure which would have seemed remarkable – perhaps even unbelievable – two decades ago. Did he really anticipate the potential of this hidden F1 asset when he bought the Brabham team in 1971?

"No, definitely not," he explained many years later. "I was not thinking in those terms at all when I bought Brabham. It was only

when I began to get fully involved in the whole scene that I appreciated just how fragmented the television coverage had been. Some
people covered a few races, some people none at all. My initial motivation was to get the whole business grouped together in an effort
to get some decent overall coverage."

By the start of 1976, the Brabham team had subtly changed its
emphasis. No longer did Ecclestone pay to use customer Cosworth
DFV engines, but instead forged a deal with Alfa Romeo to supply its
powerful, but heavy flat-12 engines. Alfa also paid handsomely for
the privilege of supplying Brabham, and the following year
Ecclestone replaced Martini as the team's title sponsor with the
Italian dairy company Parmalat. They would remain on the flanks of
the Brabhams for almost ten years.

By 1979 it was clear that Ecclestone and the FOCA-aligned
teams were in a strong position to stake a claim to a larger share of
the television income which, on the face of it, accrued to the sport's
governing body, then the Fédération Internationale du Sport
Automobile, FISA, a branch of the Fiat empire. Yet it was Bernie's
tireless efforts that had generated all this income for the sport and,
quite rightly, FOCA felt it was entitled to a larger slice of the cake.

For its part, the governing body did not like what it saw.

Ecclestone and FOCA, they reasoned, were having too much in
the way of commercial influence. The whole affair was aggravated in
1979 when the newly elected FISA President, the mercurial
Frenchman Jean-Marie Balestre, decided to take on FOCA, determined to retrieve for the FISA the notional concept of having the
"sporting power".

Ecclestone now led his FOCA-aligned teams into a battle over
the fundamental matter of who controlled motor racing. It was a turbulent period during the sport's history with some races being boycotted, others taking place outside the official World Championship.

Yet Bernie continued to remain the most influential man in the
F1 pit lane. FOCA and FISA eventually reached an accommodation

which was enshrined in the Concorde Agreement, a complex protocol of rules and regulations originally framed to control the way in which the sport was administered from a technical, financial and sporting viewpoint.

But the most important single long-term result to stem from the FOCA/FISA wars, as they became known, was the emergence of Ecclestone's legal advisor Max Mosley as one of the most influential personalities behind the scenes.

As F1 became more popular throughout the 1980s, and Ecclestone became progressively richer, so Mosley laid the foundations of his own personal challenge for power on the international motorsporting scene.

In 1991, after a carefully judged campaign, Mosley defeated Balestre for the FISA presidency. The governing body would eventually devolve the right to exploit the commercial aspects of the F1 World Championship to Ecclestone's companies, which would make him even richer in the longer term.

The Concorde Agreement was renewed several times, but by 1997 three teams – Williams, McLaren and Tyrrell – were standing out against signing a new deal, simply because they felt that Ecclestone's business organisation was taking too big a slice of the commercial cake. This provoked an impasse which took some time to resolve.

As things stood at that moment, those teams which had signed the Concorde Agreement – Ferrari, Benetton, Jordan, Sauber, Minardi, Arrows and Prost – enjoyed a seven-way split of a fixed percentage of the gross television revenue.

Eventually a new deal was formalised which provided for between $9 and $23 million dollars in annual television revenue for the 11 competing teams – with the proviso for a 12th in anticipation of Honda entering with its own factory team at the start of 2000. However, this never actually came to pass and Toyota was allowed the 12th place in the line-up in preparation for its arrival on the scene by 2002 at the latest.

This money payable to the teams under the terms of the Concorde Agreement is due whether or not the commercial rights holder – in this case Ecclestone – makes a profit or a loss on the overall operation of the various television coverage contracts through his FOCA TV organisation and associated subsidiaries.

The Concorde Agreement has gradually evolved into a three-sided commercial and sporting relationship binding the competing teams with the FIA and Ecclestone, as the F1 commercial rights holder who is licensed by the governing body to exploit the sport's commercial rights.

Mosley stated his belief that, whatever the three teams in dispute may have said, most F1 teams would be significantly better off under the terms of a proposed new Concorde Agreement.

"The changes to the division of the television money which have followed the revised Agreement have had a fundamental effect on the smaller signatory teams," said Max, "in that the amount of money they can expect to receive has been significantly increased.

"Under the previous Concorde Agreement, the FIA would make an agreement with the teams which, in turn, would reach an agreement with the commercial rights holder (Mr Ecclestone). Now, instead of a straight line, what we have is effectively a triangle. The FIA has agreements with both Mr Ecclestone and the teams. Part of each of these two agreements provides that the commercial rights holder will pay the teams the monies as laid down in the Concorde Agreement."

Yet there were two key issues that the dissenting teams continued to be worried about – and indeed continued to be worried about after the matter was resolved in the short-term. They did not believe they were receiving sufficient TV income, and they were concerned about who would run the commercial side of F1 when the time came for Bernie Ecclestone to retire.

Mosley, taking a formal tone, was reluctant to reveal what proportion of the monies was taken by Ecclestone in his role as commercial rights holder.

"It is impossible to quote the precise sums," he said briskly in 1997, "because so many of the deals are to do with television, an area which is going through significant expansion at the moment. This will be to the considerable benefit of the teams. In this area, the financial expenditure is enormous. I believe that Mr Ecclestone now has 140 people working on producing elements of the TV show, whereas in 1989 I believe there were only five.

"Notwithstanding that, the arrangement made by the teams is that they take a percentage of the gross. Two or three years ago, Mr Ecclestone made an enormous investment in digital television at a time when almost everyone was saying that he would lose every penny.

"It is now looking as though digital TV will be a great success. That's good for him, but it is even better for the teams, though, because although they took no risk at all, they do not have to meet any of the costs involved.

"It is my view that the arrangements are more than fair to the teams. The best evidence that I can offer of this is that of the 11 teams, when they were all offered the opportunity to withdraw and re-negotiate, only three did so. The teams have therefore voted by eight to three that the arrangements are fair.

"I would suggest that the reason why F1 makes such good profits is not unassociated with the fact that Bernie – in my view – is a financial genius and that he works almost 24 hours a day in making the whole F1 business succeed."

The reality was that digital TV eventually bombed into a spectacular commercial failure. It turned into F1's equivalent of the dot.com stock market bubble, with many senior figures in the sport concentrating on talking up its prospects without rationalising quite why UK viewers, for example, would be prepared to pay around 12 pounds ($19) per race for the privilege of being ersatz TV directors from the comfort of their own sofas.

The failure of the digital TV programme was the result of two catastrophically arrogant assumptions by F1's powerbrokers, supported by the team principals; namely that TV coverage of sport had an almost unlimited scope for expansion, and that F1's appeal was such that a sufficient number of viewers would pay a premium price for a premium service.

Although the terrestrial viewership would hold up well globally, by comparison with other major international sports, F1 was certainly not going to be free from the dramatic effects of the economic downturn which started in 1999.

Nevertheless, in 1997 Mosley continued to be upbeat, reasoning that there was no reason why Ecclestone should not capitalise his business on the stock exchanges of the world.

"The FIA would welcome that," he insisted, "because it would mean that every detail of the finances of F1 would be out in the open and nobody could complain. It would be to the benefit of everyone.

"We (the sport) have been going through an entrepreneurial stage which is now almost finished. The final stage is the development of pay TV and digital transmission, which is already coming. There will then be a classic management phase, at which point Bernie may decide to take his company public."

Meanwhile, Bernie continued to grow richer. In the year to March 1996 he drew Britain's largest pay packet of 55.9m pounds ($87.8m). He also hit the headlines in 1997 when it was revealed that he had made a payment of 1m pounds ($1.6m) to the Labour Party, which won that year's general election. That finished Bernie's efforts to retain a low profile and he was subjected to a barrage of media interest.

Amid allegations that the payment influenced a government decision to exclude Formula 1 for some years from a tobacco advertising ban, the embarrassed Labour Party eventually repaid him the 1m pounds. Amused commentators suggested that Bernie had won both ways – securing the delay and then getting his money back.

Not that he should worry. Since 1989 he was judged to have earned 142m pounds (some $227m) in salary and dividends from his various companies. If digital television took off, it was being speculated, he and his family trusts could be another 750m pounds ($1.2bn) richer. If only...

Yet there was a fascinating, convoluted sequence of events to follow. In October 1999 Ecclestone sold 12.5 per cent of his SLEC corporate empire – named after his Croatian model wife, Slavica Ecclestone – to Morgan Grenfell Private Equity for $374m (238m pounds). This venture capital arm of Deutsche Bank attempted to syndicate another 37.5 per cent of SLEC to other investors, but Bernie eventually sold that stake to a San Francisco-based private equity company called Hellman & Friedman for around $696m (443m pounds).

At the time, Ecclestone shrugged aside suggestions that he was trying to cash in his chips before the end of the game, and eventually wanted to sell more than 50 per cent of the business.

"I really got involved in all this because the teams wanted to know what happened if I died or I ran off," he said. "It means that instead of there being a free-for-all with everyone trying to grab shares from the (his) family, it will be stable."

Most of the money generated was intended to be used to benefit the Bambino Trust, set up for Slavica and daughters Tamara and Petra, as well as paying the interest on a $1.4 billion (891m pound), ten-year bond which he launched the previous May, through the German West LB bank, to fund the anticipated expansion of digital television Grand Prix coverage. In effect, Ecclestone was cashing in his chips to protect his family, get a one-off pay-back for his exploitation of the F1 commercial rights and allow the sport's future, hoped-for prosperity to pay off the bond.

By February 2003 the *Sunday Express* rich list had his wealth calculated – or "guestimated" – at 3.26bn pounds ($5.12bn), making him easily the richest man in the UK, although the veracity of this assessment was somewhat undermined by the *Express's* notion that he had purchased the Brabham F1 team, for 100,000 pounds ($160,000) at the start of the 1972 season from Jochen Rindt. The Austrian driver had by then been dead for over a year – and never owned Brabham anyway.

The paper also calculated that Ecclestone had 2.75bn pounds ($4.32bn) of that total held in cash, not assets, land, property or shareholdings. Yet his modest demeanour had remained essentially unchanged since his early days with Brabham. He could still be seen most days enjoying a pub lunch in Knightsbridge, just around the corner from his sumptuous business headquarters in Princes Gate, overlooking Hyde Park, which he purchased from the Saudi arms dealer Adnan Khashoggi.

Amongst the competing teams, the unspoken question being murmured was "what happens next?" This is a sensitive and extremely delicate issue.

Ecclestone, who had taken on a new lease of life since undergoing a triple heart bypass operation in 1999, stated : "I intend to run Formula 1 until I die." It would take a bold person indeed to challenge him in that assertion.

Yet the fact remained that the sale of this substantial stake of his business to Hellman & Friedman, whose previous achievements included making an $880m (560m pound) profit on a $240m (152m pound) investment in advertising agents Young & Rubicam, looked suspiciously like a first staging post on a journey to a full stock exchange flotation of Ecclestone's empire.

"Our investments fit a template," said Warren Hellman, the company's chairman. "We like businesses with a major franchise. We like businesses with a substantial cash flow and we do not like to invest in firms with a lot of fixed assets like factories or forests." Formula One Holdings clearly fitted the bill on all counts.

It promised to be a good investment, but analysts firmly believed that Bernie's autocratic, hands-on management style would need to be supplemented by a highly qualified management board capable of relating Grand Prix racing matters to City institutions.

The F1 team principals, locked in by the terms of the Concorde Agreement to be happy with their income, were certainly less than happy that Ecclestone had effectively taken out all these millions which they saw as having been earned by the sweat of their brows.

"No matter how you slice it, Bernie has channelled a huge proportion of F1 income away from the sport over the past two decades, particularly with this development," said one F1 technical director. "And that money has been lost to the sport forever. Some of us think that the balance has been tilted much too far in his favour."

So had Bernie offered sufficient assurances to the competing teams that the future management structure of Formula 1 would offer a sufficiently wide-ranging base required by a major public company? In other words, had he taken steps to ensure that F1 would no longer be a one-man band? It seemed unlikely.

"Over the many years that I've known Bernie, he has always been cautious about giving commitments and promises, but when given, they can be relied upon even though there is sometimes an impish twist to achieve a small edge in his favour," said Ron Dennis, managing director of the TAG McLaren group.

"When I look upon the last 20 years, I have mixed views about some of the outcomes of the inevitable continuous political infighting which is an inevitable part of F1. Normally the issues are very complex and Bernie is a master of the divide and rule strategy.

"That said, it is his consistent drive to improve the promotional standards and image of Grand Prix racing and driving a hard bargain in securing extremely good commercial terms for television, that has seen the popularity of the sport rise to the dizzy heights of fortnightly audiences of half a billion.

"This achievement has passed the teams not only a revenue stream (from TV) but, more importantly, has provided a strong platform from which they can derive a high level of funding from sponsors and investors who have now materialised in the form of financial institutions and automotive manufacturers."

Mosley's opinion at the time was that "we have developed quite a delicate eco-system in F1 in which everybody is inter-dependent on everybody. Bernie's recent sale represents another move towards a full flotation. But he knows that it can no longer purely be a one-man operation, and that realisation represents the transition from the entrepreneurial to managerial phase of the business. Bernie will continue to take a leading role, but he will obviously have assistance."

Mosley also believed that the success of F1 was being achieved despite the European Union continuing to investigate complaints that the television contracts were anti-competitive. "Interestingly, the interest shown in Grand Prix racing by many financial institutions does not seem to have been affected by this," he said.

Ecclestone also denied that F1 was under excessive pressure from the EU, but left Mosley to warn that the sport could remove itself almost completely from Europe unless the commission got off its back. Mosley's comments were hardly encouraging to any fund managers who might have been considering getting involved in the F1 flotation. Basically, Mosley and Ecclestone had to prove to the EU that the sporting and commercial sides of the F1 business were to be separated and not controlled by the same entity, something which the terrier-like Karel van Miert, the EU competition commissioner at that time – and a man towards whom Mosley in particular conceived a very violent dislike – was insisting upon.

In the end, the FIA agreed to lease Ecclestone the F1 commercial rights for 100 years, for a one-off payment of $300m(191m pounds) , which was used to fund the newly established FIA Foundation, and the road and racing safety initiatives which flowed from this new organisation.

Ron Dennis reflected the view of many F1 team owners who believe that any fundamental change to the structure of F1 Holdings could briefly have an adverse effect.

"As and when Bernie moves out of F1, irrespective of the structure he leaves in place, I believe there will be an initial short-term financial dip," he said. "No doubt there will be some commercial pain, but I am comfortable that ... he cares enough about F1 that, in the end, whatever mechanism or structure he leaves behind will provide for the essential commercial continuity.

"The vast majority of teams, at one stage or another, have been the recipient of Bernie's help. Fortunately for myself and McLaren, we have never needed to take advantage of that side of Bernie, because of course, being an entrepreneur, he always looks for a better-than-balanced return.

"This and other elements of his style conceal a rarely seen softer side to his personality."

Dennis was reflecting what is well known in the inner circles of Formula 1, but carefully hidden by Ecclestone from his public persona – his unpublicised help and generosity towards individuals who have fallen on hard times, in particular supporting the Spinal Injuries charity, the driving force behind which has been Professor Sid Watkins, the FIA's highly respected medical delegate and one of the world's top neurosurgeons.

Ecclestone conceded that his style may change, albeit slightly. "I am going to stand back more, perhaps go to fewer races," he said. "The trouble is that when teacher is there, people are frightened to mess it up. They are nervous of making a decisions. But I take the view that I do not mind people messing it up, as long as they make a decision."

In fact, the ownership of that share in F1 by Hellman & Friedman was brief in the extreme. Within a month, the German media company EMTV purchased both the Morgan Grenfell and Hellman & Friedman stakes for a reputed $1.5bn (955m pounds), giving both those "temporary" owners close to a 100 per cent profit.

EMTV was a family-controlled business run by Thomas Haffa which had spent $696m (443m pounds) only months before to purchase the Jim Henson company, the creators of the Muppet show. On the face of it, the deal valued the entire F1 business at $4.16bn (2.64bn pounds), half of which was owned by SLEC, the Ecclestone family trust.

In 2001 Kirch, a rival German TV media company, bought EMTV and exercised an option to purchase another 25 per cent of the F1 business from Bernie's trust for $1bn (636m pounds). Kirch would subsequently collapse, leaving bankers J P Morgan, Lehman Brothers and Bayerische Landesbank owning the 75 per cent stake.

Shortly after closing the deal with Hellman & Friedman, the spectre of Ecclestone's 1997 donation to the Labour Party erupted to embarrass the government, after Bernie slammed Tony Blair for "third-rate behaviour" in an interview in the *Sunday Times* newspaper.

Instead of keeping to the agreement they had to keep quiet about the donation – which was widely interpreted as an attempt by Bernie to buy F1 an exemption from tobacco advertising restrictions – Ecclestone said that Blair "started talking".

Ecclestone commented: "I rarely regret anything I do, but I am disappointed that Blair could not keep his word about that. I said to these clowns: if someone puts me up against the wall with a machine gun, I will not confirm or deny anything about the donation. They said, OK, OK, we will do the same. The next thing that happens is that Blair starts talking. I only found out by accident. It is third-rate behaviour."

The interview with Ecclestone and his wife Slavica came on a weekend when the pair were rated sixth equal in the always keenly awaited *Sunday Times* list of the richest 1000 people in Britain.

The *Sunday Times* Top 1000 also included many motor racing personalities, with McLaren chief Ron Dennis equal 198th on $240m (153m pounds), Tom Walkinshaw, former owner of the Arrows team, which went bankrupt in early 2003, 216th on $224m (143m pounds), Frank Williams equal 327th on $155m (99m pounds), Jackie Stewart 447th on $112m (71m pounds), Eddie Jordan 508th on $104m (66m pounds), Adrian Reynard 531st on $96m (61m pounds) – (Reynard's racing car production company went bankrupt in 2002) – and Prodrive boss David Richards, who now also runs BAR, equal 688th on $72m (46m pounds). Former F1 world champion Nigel Mansell was also there in joint 747th place on $64m (41m pounds).

Yet there was even more embarrassment for Blair over this issue later in the year, following allegations of lack of candour on the part of senior government members in a book published by British political journalist Andrew Rawnsley, entitled *Servants of the People.*

As Ecclestone arrived at Indianapolis along with FIA president Max Mosley for the inaugural United States GP to be staged at the famous American track, back in the UK the new book claimed that Blair and Chancellor Gordon Brown were not totally candid with their public utterances on the matter of Ecclestone's planned contribution. It focused on the apparent naivety of the British politicians and caused huge amusement in British motor racing circles as a result.

In November 1997, Ecclestone had said: "I met Mr Blair in July 1996 and was very impressed with him and his plans for our country. In January 1997, I was asked by a colleague to make a contribution to New Labour (Blair's party), which I did. I have never sought any favour from New Labour or any member of the government, nor has one been given."

What is clear is that Ecclestone gave Labour 1m pounds before the May 1997 election which swept Blair to power. He was in talks over another payment for the same amount, yet on 16 October 1997 he went to Downing Street with Mosley to lobby Mr Blair to exempt F1 racing from a tobacco advertising ban, arguing that as many as 40,000 jobs in the UK could be lost as teams relocated to other parts of the world.

It was alleged that no proper minutes were kept of this meeting, and on 4 November it emerged in Brussels that Britain's anti-smoking health minister Tessa Jowell was arguing for this F1 exemption. The fallout rocked the government for a week.

The salesmanship of Ecclestone and Mosley was as effective as Blair's lack of savvy proved remarkable. It seemed clear that the prime minister's office made precious little effort to verify the arguments put forward by F1's powerbrokers. A couple of phone calls would have revealed that it was nonsense to suggest that British F1 teams would relocate outside the UK – and thus Max and Bernie easily won the day.

At the end of the episode, Bernie got his tobacco exemption – and his 1 million pound contribution which was later returned on advice from the government's legal advisors – and the Blair administration was made to look extremely stupid. One was left with the inevitable thought that Ecclestone and Mosley would probably run Britain much more effectively.

One could also arguably breathe a sigh of relief that Blair and Brown were not running F1.

Materially, Ecclestone has everything he needs. A trio of US-registered private jets gleam on the tarmac at Biggin Hill, the wartime Kent fighter base which he also owns. Bernie's wry sense of self-deprecating humour is reflected in their registration numbers. N2FU is a 1990 Learjet 31, N12FU a 1994 Learjet 60 while his $26m Falcon 2000, dating from 2001, carries the identification N999BE. Think about them all. Very carefully.

Learjet N12FU was eventually sold to the FIA in 2002 and is now registered N69LJ, remaining on the US register. It is now used by FIA president Max Mosley.

Bernie and his statuesque wife Slavica, a former Emporio Armani model whom he first met at Monza in 1982 before she could even speak a word of English, have an ocean-going yacht which is based for much of its time in the Adriatic, close to Mrs Ecclestone's roots in Croatia. They have two daughters, Tamara, now 19, and Petra, now 16, on whom they dote.

The signs are already that Milan-born Tamara has inherited her parents' independent streak. Having been coaxed into attending the

Crillon Haute Couture ball in Paris just before Christmas 2001, she told the *Sunday Times*: "With all the tantrums and egos, headaches and famous names, the ball was very much like another world with which I'm familiar – one that uses carbon-fibre instead of silk."

By any standards Ecclestone is a fascinating character. He can be a ruthless negotiator – a role which he clearly relishes – deploying a brain power and intellect which few can rival in any business sphere.

Just do not cross him.

06: MAX ATTACK; THE MOSLEY BOY

As Ecclestone rode the crest of the commercial wave which carried F1 to its current position of global sporting pre-eminence, he was ably assisted by another extraordinary individual, the son of the British Fascist leader, who gave up a brilliant career as a lawyer to become involved in motor racing.

Max Mosley played the "long game" exceptionally well to become president of the FIA, motor racing's governing body, and a leading light in European Union politics. Astute, cool, calculating and extremely intelligent, he has been the ideal administrative mastermind.

When he started March Engineering in 1970, his father Sir Oswald commented wryly: "You'll almost certainly go bust, but it will be good training for something serious later on." Sir Oswald, who died in 1980 at the age of 84, was right on the money.

Mosley's father was one of the most controversial personalities in 20th century British political history. When he died in 1980, many newspapers found it difficult to say much that was complimentary about him.

Yet in many ways, he was a visionary. If you set aside his disastrous decision to found the British Union of Fascists – and his apparent alignment with Hitler's ambitions – Oswald Mosley was regarded by some, at least in his earlier years, as politically imaginative. To take a single example, he was one person keen on a united Europe. And that was decades before the Common Market officially came into being.

Max Mosley has certainly inherited much of his father's charisma and energy. Thankfully, he is somewhat less controversial than his parent, although the F1 team principals increasingly believe that the emphasis should very definitely be on the "somewhat".

Many within Formula 1, for example, still regard him as something of a radical. Either way, he is certainly firmly in charge in his role as FIA president and seems to have an insatiable appetite for more of the same.

Now 63, Mosley is remarkably youthful. He likes nothing better than a stimulating intellectual discussion, although often he clearly finds it difficult to demonstrate sufficient patience with the views of some F1 team principals. He is hugely energetic and still loves snowboarding with a passion. He professes to being "fundamentally quite lazy", an assertion which nobody believes for a moment.

Mosley seems anxious that everybody's voice should be heard, but he is not a man who suffers fools gladly. One gets the strong impression that he wants his own voice to be heard over the general hubbub and din generated by the F1 business, on and off the track. Like Ecclestone, he has a well-honed strain of self-deprecatory humour which he often deploys to get himself off the hook on the occasions he is close to losing an argument. He worked for a decade to achieve his current position at the top of international motorsport and has no intention of allowing that toil to be squandered.

Max Rufus Mosley was the second son of Sir Oswald's much publicised marriage to Diana Guinness, one of the famous Mitford sisters, who hit the headlines of London society in 1933 when she left her husband, the Hon. Bryan Guinness, to set up house with the maverick politician.

Their youngest son was born in 1940, just weeks before Diana and her husband were imprisoned under the controversial wartime emergency regulation 18B in 1940 as suspected security risks. Between 1945 and '53, Max lived with his parents in France and Ireland, educated partly at home in Ireland and sometimes let off lessons by his father in order that he could concentrate on his hunting, a great passion in his early teenage years. He was later educated at Stein an der Traun, Germany. He recalled: "I also got expelled from one school following a slight misunderstanding with a teacher who found me in the girls' dormitory."

By all accounts, Max and his older brother Alexander were both a bit of a handful. In Jan Dalley's biography of their mother (*Diana Mosley. A Life*, published by Faber and Faber, 1999), a friend of the family recounted that their father Sir Oswald always tacitly encouraged them in fights with older boys from the village when they lived in rural Wiltshire just after the war. They certainly inherited a wild and independent streak from their individualistic parents.

Dalley's book also contains a photograph of Sir Oswald passionately haranguing a crowd in Trafalgar Square during the early days of the British Union of Fascists – intriguingly just below the third floor window of the FIA Foundation offices now occupied by his youngest son. One is drawn to the conclusion that Sir Oswald was debating issues other than Formula 1 traction control systems and the Concorde Agreement.

Max became secretary of the prestigious Oxford Union during his university education at Christ Church and went on to become a barrister, being called to the Bar in 1964, after which he specialised in the complexities of patent and trademark law. But it was not enough.

"One day, walking through Middle Temple, it struck me that, if I could stick this out for 40 years, I might become a senior, respected barrister and might even become a judge," he said.

"But I'd be stuck in court on hot summer days, having to wear a suit. I reckoned there had to be something better to do."

He has admitted that, to some degree, he went racing because it was something he could do on his own terms without the residual baggage of his surname.

He was hooked when his wife Jean, whom he had married in 1960 when they were both Oxford undergraduates, was given tickets for a race at Silverstone. He admitted that he was transfixed by the sight of the cars swooping around Woodcote corner, then an absolutely flat-out right-hander before the pits: "I knew this was something I absolutely had to do."

Mosley once memorably recalled an occasion when he was competing in a club race meeting at a small provincial British track during 1967. He was in a crush of drivers straining to read their lap times, which had been posted on a board outside the race control office.

"Mosley, hmm Mosley," said a voice thoughtfully. Max froze, wondering whether the inevitable connection would be made. Then the voice continued: "I wonder if that's a relative of Alf Mosley, the coachbuilder?"

Max was a highly competitive Clubmans racer and his U2 was always immaculately prepared in its light blue livery. He raced wheel-to-wheel with 22-year-old Howard Heerey's Chevron B2 in the battle for the Clubmans' title, eventually won by Heerey, who scored 21 race wins.

Such was the level of competition that Heerey and Mosley once collided battling for the lead at Croft, another small British track, but generally their rivalry was clean and sporting. By current F1 standards, at least.

Mosley even stripped the U2 of its mudguards and entered it into the Formula 2 international race at Crystal Palace, one of the blue riband international events on the British motor racing calendar. This was the 1960s equivalent of running a 4-year-old Formula 3000 car in the 2003 Monaco Grand Prix. Max was totally outclassed and failed to qualify for the final, which was won by future Ferrari driver Jacky Ickx in a Matra MS7 entered by Ken Tyrrell.

Mosley graduated from Clubmans racing to compete in the International Formula 2 series in 1968. He bought a Brabham BT23C – very much the "customer car" of its time – and was partnered with fellow Brabham driver Chris Lambert under the title London Racing Team.

Mosley's maiden F2 outing was at Hockenheim on 7 April. He qualified way down the grid for the first of the two 20-lap heats, finishing ninth on aggregate, two laps down on the winning Matra of Jean-Pierre Beltoise. It was the race at which the brilliant Jim Clark was killed, and it made a huge impact on Mosley.

Max was in the thick of the midfield F2 action at the traditional Easter Monday Thruxton International when his Brabham stopped with a broken valve. He failed to qualify for the final at Crystal Palace, finished eighth in the Monza Lottery where Jean-Pierre Jaussaud's Tecno flipped and burnt out in front of him, after which his team-mate Lambert was killed in a violent smash after a controversial collision with Clay Regazzoni's Tecno.

To this day, Mosley keeps a 32-year-old copy of the Italian sports magazine *Il Giorno* in a corner of his office. Dominating its front page is a photograph of Jaussaud's blazing Tecno at Monza with Mosley's Brabham passing in the foreground.

"Each time I went past it, I could feel the heat from the fire," he recalled. "I remember resolving when I was racing in F2 that if I ever got into any position of authority within the sport, I would try to reverse the 'if you do not like it, you do not have to do it' and 'if you think a corner is dangerous, just slow down' which is all nonsense.

Max had been FIA president for nine years when, in 2000, he told me about a copy letter he had recently received from his 90-year-old mother Diana in Paris. "It contained a letter I'd written to her in 1968 recounting a dinner when I was exchanging funny stories with

Jochen Rindt and Piers Courage, mainly about a third driver who will be nameless.

"I mentioned to my mother in this letter than it was slightly depressing that they were all younger than me. I was 28 at the time and all three of them – Rindt, Courage and the other driver – were dead before the time they were 30. That's how it was, absolutely horrific." He added: "So, sometimes drivers come in here to talk about safety and sometimes I say to them 'that's not dangerous, this is dangerous' and show them the newspaper cover from that race in 1968."

Later tragedy would touch Mosley as a team principal when Roger Williamson was killed in the works March 731 in the 1973 Dutch Grand Prix. "I had to tell his father, who doted on him," he reflected. "It was awful.

"Competing in F1 during the 1960s and early 1970s was like being in a front-line regiment during a major war. You just lost contemporary after contemporary. But, of course, while it is difficult to imagine a war taking place without people getting killed, it's perfectly possible to have motorsport where people do not get killed.

"Moreover, motorsport generally is much more popular amongst the wider, non-enthusiast public than it ever was when it was so very dangerous."

Mosley's own racing career ended in 1969 after his Lotus spun off at the Nurburgring. History recalls him as a journeyman driver, yet Brian Hart, the respected F1 engine builder and then a very competitive F2 driver, is more complimentary.

"I reckon Max was alright as a racer in that Brabham," he said in 2003. "He might not have been particularly quick, but he was a thinking driver. He kept out of trouble and generally used his head." Later Hart would supply the March team's F2 engines and found Mosley "a joy to work with, no problem at all. Max paid promptly and was absolutely brilliant."

Mosley kept his Brabham F2 car in a lock-up garage at Slough, near London's Heathrow Airport. He shared it with a character by the name of Frank Williams who was fielding a similar car for Eton-educated racer Piers Courage, a member of the famous brewing family.

Frank had lofty plans to move into Grand Prix racing the following year. One day he asked Mosley whether he had got a degree in physics. Mosley said, yes, as a matter of fact he had.

"So you know about the technicalities of building racing cars," Williams continued. Not really, Max told him. Williams then asked whether he thought he could pretend that he knew. "I suppose so," said Max.

What Frank had in mind was for Max to accompany him to the headquarters of the Reynolds aluminium company in the USA to make a pitch for sponsorship. Max was being offered a small commission if the deal came off. So he prepared his brief in meticulous detail, like a good barrister should. At the meeting, he did most of the talking. Reynolds were impressed and eventually agreed that it would be a good idea if they got involved in F1 sponsorship. Which they did. With McLaren.

But the exercise had been sufficient to convince Max that he had the gift of the gab when it came to chatting up potential sponsors. He proved it when arranging the backing from American oil additive company STP for the works March F1 team in 1970.

That season, Mosley and his colleagues would run the works F1 March team for Chris Amon and Jo Siffert, and also private cars for Ronnie Peterson and Mario Andretti. They sold cars to top team owner Ken Tyrrell for Jackie Stewart, Johnny Servoz-Gavin and later François Cevert.

Yet the March directors were not the most astute businessmen. They struggled to keep afloat, despite selling a lot of cars. Financial margins were tight and the March 701 was not a particularly good racing car.

Tyrrell realised that early on and started building his own machine within weeks of Stewart's first race outing in the March. The following year March lost 71,000 pounds. "This was a simply massive sum in those days," said Max. "Far beyond our personal means."

Mosley arranged a line of credit with a merchant bank through his step-brother Jonathan Guinness, and took complete control of the financial side of the business. Alan Rees left the team soon afterwards.

Eventually Max would retire from March in 1977 and sell his shareholding. "The business no longer really had any need for me and I'd really run out of enthusiasm for it," he said.

Reflecting on those years with March, Max has very specific memories. "March was started just as the big motor industry spending of the 1969s was coming to an end," he recalled, "but before the advent of the pure advertising sponsor in F1.

"There was never enough income, nor did we have anything approaching the amount of capital needed. The business was a financial puzzle from day one.

"Everything we did has to be seen in the context of this acute lack of cash. Probably the worse aspect was that we never found out what Robin (Herd) might have done in the early 1970s had he been given the financial resources to develop his ideas fully.

"We did, however, begin the process which led to the development of modern Grand Prix racing. Some rounds of the 1969 World Championship had only 13 cars. All this changed in 1970, with ten March Formula 1 cars built, and usually five or six of them on the grid.

"In addition, everyone could see that there was nothing magic about Formula 1. If we could start in September with an empty shed and no money, yet be on the front row of the grid the following March, so could they.

"Of course, this was only possible because we were fortunate enough to assemble an extraordinarily able group of helpers. They achieved an astonishing amount in the early days, working day and night under great pressure. Most of them are still in the motor racing business and now occupy very senior positions."

Political acumen has increasingly become a key requirement for anybody involved in professional sport. Max had it in spades and as

Formula 1 accelerated into the fast lane in terms of growth and international popularity during the 1970s, there was clearly huge potential for anybody with a keen intellect.

Moreover, Mosley had forged a shrewd personal relationship with Ecclestone. The eloquent former lawyer with the gregarious nature might have seemed an unlikely associate for the secretive, distant former car dealer, but they quickly learned they could play to each other's strengths.

"Bernie instinctively knew that Max was extremely clever and excellent when it came to planning and organisation," said one of their close collaborators from that era. "They quickly became two parts of the same personality, if you like. Yet you are never quite sure. Are they partners, or do they have their own separate agendas for Formula 1. Whatever the truth of it, they have kept us guessing ever since the early 1980s."

The author first met Max in June 1970, when I accompanied my *Motoring News* colleague Andrew Marriott to the March factory on Launton Road industrial estate at Bicester, near Oxford. Marriott was a close friend of all the directors and as he went off to chat with them, I was told to "wander around" and have a look at the place.

So I duly "wandered around" and during the course of my self-directed tour, I stumbled into a smaller workshop where the first of the following year (1971) March 712M Formula 2 cars was being constructed. Suddenly I found myself confronted by this sandy-haired, I might say skinny, young man. "Can I ask you what are you doing in here?" said the future FIA president crisply. I explained who I was and who I'd come with. It seemed at least sufficient to avoid summary execution.

"Oh well, if you don't mind coming out of this area," he said. "You see, we're busy with some high-technology future projects and it's all very confidential." He ushered me politely away. Over the years, I meant to ask him what these confidential high-tech projects really were. I suppose he meant the new March F2 car. If so, his salesmanship was matched only by his crust.

Max would spend much of the 1980s out of sight of the F1 teams. After the FOCA/FISA wars at the turn of that decade – where the Grand Prix teams and the governing body under the presidency of Jean-Marie Balestre fought long and hard over the right to control the sport's lucrative cash base – Mosley had other things on his mind.

After his father's death there was time spent sorting out Sir Oswald's estate. Then between 1982 and 1985 he took three years away from motor racing during which time he seriously probed the possibility of a career in UK politics. That process included conversations with Tory grandee Lord Stockton, the former prime minister Harold Macmillan, who advised him that the Mosley surname would still probably represent an insuperable handicap at the ballot box.

Circumstances conspired to give me the chance of watching Mosley in action. During 1980 I worked briefly for the CSS sports promotion company and – for reasons which are lost to me over the passage of the years – found myself taking dictation from Mosley at the 1980 Spanish Grand Prix as he lit the fuse which was to set F1 aflame with controversy for the next two seasons.

Throughout the 1970s, the Formula One Constructors' Association had become a powerful force under the presidency of Bernie Ecclestone. Its rise to prominence might well have been ignored for the most part by the sport's administrators, the Commission Sportive Internationale (CSI) which later changed its title to the Fédération Internationale du Sport Automobile (FISA). But if, during that period, you were a race organiser, then the only person you had to speak to was Bernie Ecclestone.

Ecclestone organised the financial arrangements for the races on behalf of the team owners. Organisers did not pay out on a published prize scale, they handed the whole amount over to FOCA, which then distributed it amongst its members by means of a complex, secret formula.

It had almost got to the point where FISA was effectively being bypassed by the commercially astute Ecclestone. For legal, administrative and historic reasons it certainly sanctioned the races, but its authority had been progressively diluted by the time the volatile Jean-Marie Balestre was elected FISA President at the end of 1978. From the very start of his tenure, it was clear that his spell in command was going to be different.

At a stroke, FOCA's unimpeded push towards overall F1 dominance seemed to have been checked. Balestre was an eccentric extrovert who seemed to like nothing better than playing the Napoleonic card. But, as Mosley and Ecclestone quickly appreciated, he was no fool.

Born in 1920, Balestre enjoyed a colourful and action-packed career. He served in the French Resistance during the war and carried out covert activities against the German forces in his occupied land. When, in the late 1970s, photographs began to circulate of Balestre apparently wearing a German uniform, he took unsuccessful legal action to prevent their publication.

He explained that he was a double agent who had been ordered to infiltrate the enemy and insists that he was once arrested by the Gestapo, tortured and condemned to death. Only the Allied invasion saved him.

During the post-war years he helped found an important Paris-based publishing group and the FFSA (Fédération Française du Sport Automobile) in 1952, at a time when a handful of regional race organising clubs dominated the administration of French motorsport.

Balestre was also an aggressively competitive journalist and publisher. His criticism of some French road cars of the time incensed the manufacturers. Moreover, when plans for the new Citroën DS19 went astray, the car maker sent the police into his office in search of them. Balestre certainly was not afraid of a fight.

In his new role as FISA President, Balestre played hardball from the start. At the first race of the 1979 season, John Watson's

McLaren M28 tangled with Jody Scheckter's Ferrari 312T3 and caused the race to be flagged to a halt. Watson suspects that Balestre's robust intervention may have been behind the stewards' decision to penalise him with a draconian fine.

In 1980, Balestre announced that the following season would see the banning of sliding aerodynamic side-skirts on F1 cars. These were the key to the effectiveness of ground-effect aerodynamics which had been pioneered in 1976/77 by Lotus and further refined to competitive heights by Williams and Brabham.

The British teams seethed at what they regarded as a decision deliberately to handicap their efforts. The FOCA members were pre-dominantly the British-based specialist F1 teams. They relied on their own technical chassis ingenuity to get the best out of Cosworth-Ford DFV engine performance, at a time when the FIA-aligned Ferrari and Renault teams were pressing ahead with their more powerful turbocharged engines.

Finally, at the 1980 Monaco Grand Prix came an incident which triggered the first round of the in-fighting. At the start of the season, it had been agreed that a compulsory drivers' briefing would take place at every race. But at Zolder, venue for the Belgian Grand Prix a couple of weeks before Monaco, and then at Monaco again, a handful of drivers were told by their team bosses not to attend. They were also assured that FOCA would take care of any penalties that might arise.

Inevitably the drivers were fined for their indiscipline. Payment was not forthcoming. Balestre then responded with the predictable statement that if those concerned did not pay up, their international racing licences would be suspended prior to the Spanish Grand Prix on 1 June.

FOCA, led by Ecclestone with Mosley at his elbow, now played what they believed would be their ace. Having effectively manipulated their way into a set-piece confrontation with the governing body, the British teams announced that – unless Balestre quashed the fines – then they would not be competing at Jarama.

Understandably, at this point the Spanish race organisers intervened. All they wanted to do was to protect the future of their event, and they were not really interested in the wider political firestorm which was poised to engulf the sport.

The Real Automóvil Club de España (RACE) volunteered to deposit the entire sum of the outstanding fines with the FISA. No, that would not do at all, responded Balestre. The drivers concerned had to pay the penalties personally.

The RACE then came up with a novel solution – or, rather, Mosley and Ecclestone gave them a nudge in the ribs with an apparent formula to get everybody off the hook. They decided to run the race under the auspices of the FIA – the parent organisation of which the FISA was a constituent component – in the belief that this could legally and effectively bypass Balestre's authority. The F1 constructors energetically agreed with this stance.

The mechanics of the situation were bafflingly complex. RACE, which acted as the organising club, had delegated their sporting powers to the Federación Española de Automovilismo (FEA), but on the Friday morning of the race weekend, RACE reclaimed their authority, a move which Balestre's FISA regime regarded as unconstitutional.

The upshot of all this was that on the Friday of the race weekend, I found myself cast in the unlikely role of Max Mosley's impromptu private secretary. As I later recalled in *F1 Racing* magazine, it is not very often you get asked to do this job – and then get Bernie Ecclestone to hand out the press release which is the end result of one's labours.

The previous evening, Max had spent just about every waking hour drafting FOCA's position in this confrontation. Dissatisfied with his efforts so far, he had risen from his bed in the small hours of the morning and re-written the draft statement in the form of questions and answers, a device he employs regularly to this day in his role as FIA president.

Max arrived in the caravan and told me: "We've got to write it again." This was a euphemism for *you've* got to *type* it again. I blurted indignantly: "But I've already written this out twice."

In crisply precise tones, Max replied: "Well, you'll just have to do it again, won't you?" The modulation of his voice suggested that this was not a matter for lengthy debate. I was not being asked for my opinion.

The upshot of all this was that it was announced that the FISA officials would no longer be required at Jarama. Somewhat theatrically, they were escorted to the circuit gates by armed guards and sent packing.

Come the start of practice on Friday morning, the mood in the pit lane was one of thinly suppressed mischief. Only Ferrari, Renault, Alfa Romeo and the private Williams FW07 of local hero Emilio de Villota ventured out onto the circuit for the first half-hour. Then the session was red-flagged to a halt and the FOCA-inspired, "FIA approved" regime began.

At this point the three "grandee" teams – Ferrari, Renault and Alfa Romeo – decided to play no further part in the weekend. They could see that because of their companies' involvement in other forms of motorsport, they could not risk a head-on clash with FISA.

The rest of the day was taken up with further debate behind closed doors. The Brabham and Williams mechanics played football on the start/finish straight. Ferrari and Renault did lunch, something they tended to do best in those days. The rest of the F1 fraternity simply kicked its heels and waited for something to happen.

Strange to relate that, after all that, the Spanish Grand Prix turned out to be quite a good race, championship status or not. It was dominated by Alan Jones's Williams FW07, and beating the hell out of anything French seemed to be the British team's number one priority at the time.

Since there were no Renaults in the race, they took satisfaction from seeing off the two Ligiers instead. The following week Jones summed up the situation in his column for *Motor* magazine, now long defunct. "My job is to drive racing cars, not to get involved in politics," he said rather simplistically.

"As far as I'm concerned, the Spanish Grand Prix was no different from normal. As it happened, I won the race, and now I have to wait and see if I'll be given the points."

He was not. Balestre saw to that. The FISA president, who had been holed up in a Madrid hotel for much of the weekend, left Spain on the Sunday evening bound for a meeting of the FIA in Athens the following day.

Mosley recalls: "Knowing what Balestre was up to, Bernie and I decided we had to get to Athens. There were no direct flights to anywhere near Athens from Madrid, but Bernie managed to persuade a businessman who was flying to Riyadh, in Saudi Arabia, in his private jet to drop us off in Athens. We arrived there at about two o'clock the following morning – to the horror of Balestre and his colleagues."

Max also remembered that they met up with an Italian journalist who in turn befriended the girl in charge of the telex room at the hotel where the FISA officials were staying.

"The hotel made three copies of each telex they sent," he said. "So we were in a position where we knew exactly what FISA was doing in terms of communications with the outside world." That said, it did not do FOCA much good in the short term, although Mosley believes it was a seminal moment in the relationship between the teams and the governing body.

"The whole issue at Jarama was a symbolic gesture," he remembers, "the start of the long FOCA/FISA wars. FISA may have appeared to have had the force of legality behind them as the sport's rulers, but the way in which they framed the regulations left the FOCA teams no choice but to fight.

"As Bernie was fond of saying at the time, 'If we don't hang together, we'll all hang separately.'"

More significantly, the Jarama episode indicated just what a deft negotiator Max Mosley could be. It was an instructive lesson which Formula1 would be reminded of more than a decade later.

07: WATCH YOUR BACKS; INFILTRATING THE TEAMS

Max Mosley spent around 5000 pounds on racing his Brabham BT23C in the European F2 series during the summer of 1968. "That was the equivalent of being able to do Formula 3000 for 60,000 pounds in 2002," he reflected.

Yet by 2002, Formula 3000 budgets were nudging the million-pound mark, admittedly for two cars. "I mean, what I spent on F2 would be a good international karting budget these past few years," said Max. "Costs have gone wildly out of control and it's just not sustainable."

Max was speaking at the start of the 2003 season in the weeks after he had effectively imposed the FIA's dramatic programme of cost-cutting measures on the F1 teams. He was not seeking to address the disparity between the performance of the good cars and bad cars; that is just a fact of life in motor racing. More the disparity between the amount of money which was being, in his view, wasted by the top teams in order to sustain their pre-eminence. Spending one's way to victory was creating an untenable situation, if perhaps a hard habit to break.

This balance between income and expenditure has always been one of the more vexed issues in the F1 business. Historically the teams have either been arguing with the organisers over money, or the organisers have been complaining that the teams have been screwing them over. Or, more recently, the teams have been complaining that they were ripped off by Ecclestone over the terms of the Concorde Agreement. Despite the fact that they voluntarily signed up for the deal.

So how did Ecclestone come to be president of the Formula One Constructors' Association in the early 1970s and use this as his powerbase for taking over the commercial side of the sport?

The answer is simple, of course. In effect, he said to the teams: "Leave all the commercial negotiating to me and I will make you as rich as Croesus." Which he did. Although what he may have neglected to say was that the formula he had in mind would make him as rich as Croesus's private bankers.

"Back in the late 1960s we had the F1 Constructors and Entrants' Association which was run by Andrew Ferguson (the former Lotus team manager) as a part-time job," recalls Mosley.

"They had meetings in the autumn of 1969, to which we were not invited because at that time most people didn't believe we had produced a car, but once we'd produced the first March 701, I got invited to a meeting, an expedition to Brussels with all the team principals to go and negotiate with the CSI (the sport's governing body).

"In those days the CSI, the promoters and the organisers were a very cosy private club and we were trying to negotiate with them collectively, but because none of the teams trusted each other, we decided to pile onto a plane and go there as a bunch. All the obvious people – Peter Warr (Lotus), Tim Parnell (BRM), Rob Walker, Frank Williams and so on. In those days, of course, Ferrari was far too grand to have anything to do with all this.

"I was invited along partly because we were ready at March with our first cars and partly because I was a barrister and they thought I might be useful to have around.

"So I am sitting in this first meeting thinking 'this is a major world sport, I can't believe what I (am) witnessing.' I couldn't believe that it could be run like that. It just wasn't possible."

During the course of the '71 season, Bernie Ecclestone duly appeared as a potential purchaser for the Brabham F1 team. "I can remember our first meeting as if it was yesterday," said Mosley. "It was at the Excelsior Hotel near Heathrow and he quickly moved around the table to sit next to me as we were discussing some specific issue or another. And it didn't take long for the two of us to start negotiating on behalf of the teams with the organisers and promoters.

"Bernie was an ace negotiator. I learned all the tricks of the trade from him. One of those was that, if one wanted to adjourn a meeting for a private discussion, my technique was to politely offer to leave the room and leave the other side to consider its position.

"Bernie's strategy was to force the other side to leave the room so that he could rifle through the wastepaper basket and read all the notes they'd written to each other while they were negotiating."

It was clear, even at that stage, that Ecclestone was the most astute player amongst the F1 team principals. "He was absolutely in another league," said Mosley. "That was immediately obvious from the moment you started to discuss what you might do, let alone actually start doing it.

"I'll always remember there was a bomb scare at the Excelsior and we all trooped out into the car park from our ground-floor conference room. We arrived to find Bernie already there. We'd all wandered out through the reception area, which was probably the place that any bomb was about to go off, whereas Bernie had worked all that out and simply stepped through the sliding window at the end of the room and was outside before any of the rest of us. It was very clear how his mind operated."

As early as 1973 it was evident that the F1 teams were shaping up for a battle with the Grand Prix organisers over the question of their income levels. Looking back through the magazines of the time makes instructive reading.

The 4 January 1973 issue of *Motoring News* highlighted a problem under the heading "No F1 agreement in sight" on its front page. This reported on a meeting between the Formula 1 Association – the forerunner of FOCA – and Grand Prix International, a recently formed cartel of race organisers. But in their statement you could detect the first hint of Bernie's coordinating influence behind the scenes.

It was stated that as the Association was still not in agreement with GPI, it would have to negotiate individually with the European organisers. Terms had already been agreed with the Argentine, Brazilian and South African organisers for an average purse of 110,000 pounds ($176,000) per race.

This was reportedly 25,000 pounds ($40,000) more than was originally requested, and 32,000 pounds ($51,000) more than a concessionary offer of 78,000 pounds ($124,800) per race made to the European organisers through GPI. However, GPI's members were standing firm on an offer of 42,000 pounds ($67,200) per race.

All the F1 team managers argued they were losing money and that sponsorship was "not perks, but sheer necessity". Lotus team manager Peter Warr also added that in 1970 the teams had taken a cut in money to ensure the long-term future of Grand Prix racing, but GPI "merely continues to strangle our future".

A fortnight later came a headline which could well have been referring to any number of subsequent occasions over the next 30 years. It was announced that the CSI (then the FIA's motor racing arm) had decided "in principle" to make new regulations to reduce the cornering speeds of F1 cars.

Within a few more weeks came the news that Graham Hill, the hugely popular twice-world champion who was by then in the twilight of his F1 career, had been invited to become a PR ambassador for the European rounds of the World Championship, working for Grand Prix International.

Although in a lengthy interview Hill did not seem to have a terribly precise and focused concept of what his new role involved, it was clear that GPI felt it had gained the upper hand in these negotiations. The F1 teams, it seemed, were on the back foot.

In reality, the organisers never managed to organise themselves into a cohesive and consistently reliable negotiating body. Ecclestone and FOCA had the momentum with them during the early 1970s, Bernie having correctly identified that controlling and steering the teams was the key to controlling F1. It was not like golf, where the likes of Mark McCormack realised that the players were the most crucial element. At the end of the day, in F1 the teams could control the drivers, even if that mean bullying and intimidating them into toeing the line.

By 1975, the F1 constructors were seriously tightening their hold on the sport's commercial development. Yet the FIA would always be on hand to prod and provoke the team owners. In the run-up to the '75 Dutch Grand Prix, and perhaps prompted by the terrible accident at Barcelona where Rolf Stommelen's Hill-Cosworth had vaulted the safety barrier in the Spanish Grand Prix, the governing body decided that it needed to grasp the safety nettle.

Yet it did so in a haphazard and vague manner. It published a short communiqué entitled "The Evolution of Formula 1" which blamed what it judged was the out-of-hand development of wings and tyres as "major contributors to the dramatic increase in cornering forces which thus increase the danger".

The tyre companies and car designers were outraged. Goodyear pointed out that "whatever you do, people are eventually going to get their downforce back. That's what making racing cars is all about. There's only one way of making cars slower; run them with 1-litre engines and the current weight limit." It was a tongue-in-cheek response, in effect, to a set of proposals which were not being taken very seriously.

Hand-in-hand with this tradition of the FIA poking its nose into matters which the constructors believed were their own – a tradition which Max Mosley would loyally uphold after his poacher-turned-gamekeeper transformation into the FIA president from 1991 – Ecclestone was also edging towards more wide-ranging control over race contracts and prize funds.

Since 1972 the F1 constructors had been negotiating on a package deal basis, whereby the race organisers received a guaranteed number of cars turning up for their events for a set price. More crucially, this stability made F1 look a generally more appealing sport to the paying and viewing public, and as that popularity was enhanced, so Ecclestone could raise the bargaining stakes with those organisers. And this generally went off without a hitch.

By 1975 the price of a Grand Prix in Europe had been raised from $147,200 to $240,000. The plan was for this to be increased to $264,000 per race in 1977 and then to $304,000 by 1978. In addition, Ecclestone had very shrewdly factored in bonuses of 7.5 per cent based on the previous year's figure, plus the rise in the European cost of living. This was audacious stuff indeed for FOCA to be bouncing off race organisers who had traditionally held the whip hand when it came to negotiating the terms for participation in their events.

However, the two North American races were used to negotiating with FOCA on a separate basis. Between them in 1974, the US Grand Prix at Watkins Glen and the Canadian GP at Mosport Park had paid the teams $440,000 plus transportation, but that joint figure was increased to $500,000 in 1975.

The deadline for agreeing this deal was the Saturday before the German Grand Prix. The Canadians, however, were slow off the mark in agreeing and the F1 teams called off their participation in that particular race. The Canadian promoters, businessmen Bernie Kaimin and Harvey Hudes, flew to the following Austrian Grand Prix to beg their case with Ecclestone. But he was unrelenting. FOCA meant business and the teams were in business, pure and simple. So the Canadian race was cancelled, interestingly without the FIA offering a word on the issue, in one direction or another.

Significantly, by 1975 the commercial basis of distributing the F1 prize money was evolving into a structured and carefully calculated formula which would provide the basis for the commercial side of the first Concorde Agreement, by this stage still five years away in the future.

The prize fund was split into two separate sections, say – because it has never been revealed officially – 65/35 per cent. A certain proportion of the 35 per cent would be paid to the top 20 runners in the Constructors' Championship, but running on the basis of June to June, from the middle of one season to the middle of the next. The remainder of that 35 per cent was paid to the top 20 qualifiers in the race.

Meanwhile the 65 per cent share was divided on a similar basis, but only in relation to the results of the race, including a sliding scale of awards which pays up on race order at one quarter, half and three quarters distance. It was, of course, still possible for a driver to qualify 21st, finish 21st and not earn a dollar. His rivals would, of course, say that he and his team were out of their league. This would be a theme that would resurface time and again over the decades to follow.

There was one ultimate intangible, of course, the issue of the F1 commercial rights and how they were actually established as a notional commodity which could be devolved by the sport's governing body to Ecclestone as the so-called "commercial rights holder."

This was a key issue which originally set the FIA on a head-on collision course with European Union functionaries in the late 1990s as the whole issue of dividing commercial from sporting rights was scrutinised at great length and in minute detail.

Mosley explained it thus: "This is the central question to the way F1 operates and was central to our negotiations with Brussels. Before the teams started negotiating as a body, each team would do a separate deal with a race organiser for it to turn up at an individual race.

"If it was a non-Championship event, it was a straightforward commercial deal: how much is it worth to you to bring your car to run at my non-championship event? In those days organisers could pay enough in relation to the overall cost of F1 to make it viable."

Mosley was referring to the 1960s and '70s when there were several non-Championship races on the UK calendar, for example. The Race of Champions at Brands Hatch, the Silverstone International Trophy, the Aintree 200 and the Oulton Park Gold Cup were all F1 races which supplemented the British Grand Prix on the international schedule. However, in 1983 the final running of the Race of Champions rang down the curtain on the era of the non-title F1 event.

"If it was a World Championship event, however, you needed to be there to score points, of course," he continued. "And the organiser was able to use the fact that it was a Championship event to say to the leading teams 'I know you've got to come, so I won't give you much money.' So because he was a Championship event organiser, he was able to do a blinding deal.

"So then, it followed from this that, if you had a round of the World Championship, you could stage a race more cheaply than a non-championship event, and the more popular the World Championship became, the truer that became.

"So who decides whether or not you can have a World Championship round? The FIA. So, in the final analysis, the FIA is giving the organisers the means of making this money. Therefore the right to do that or not do that is extremely valuable, and those are the commercial rights to the F1 World Championship."

The first Concorde Agreement was for four years and in it, the teams acknowledged that the sport's commercial rights belonged to the governing body, but the FIA then ceded these back to the teams for four years from 1980. Balestre's idea was that these would revert to the FIA and the old system would be reintroduced.

The Concorde Agreement was then renewed for two years until the end of 1986, then there was a five-year renewal from 1987 to '92, then another five-year stint to 1997. At which point Mosley, who was by now FIA president, began to feel that the Agreement had out-lived its usefulness, becoming something of a double-edged sword.

It was at this point that the McLaren, Williams and Tyrrell teams decided to take a robust stand. They were not prepared to sign up again for another five-year term unless there was a more generous provision for directing more of the sport's income into their coffers.

Although the three teams initially withheld their signatures, Mosley was confident at the time that these were short-term problems which would soon be sorted out and that F1 racing could look forward to a healthy, expanding future. He was right and wrong in equal measure. The dissenting teams eventually signed a revised Concorde Agreement, but they were not totally satisfied that they had got a fair deal out of it.

The immediate main issue was whether or not the three dissenting teams could be readmitted from their position on the outer fringes of the F1 business as signatories to the Concorde Agreement. Mosley expressed the view that this could be possible, even though it would require a vote of approval from the existing signatories before any such restoration was accepted.

"There is to be a procedure to allow teams which have not yet signed the Agreement to become signatories," he explained. "This will involve a secret ballot of the signatory teams. If no-one is opposed, the applicant will immediately be recognised as a signatory team. The secrecy is to avoid any embarrassment.

"It means, of course, that a new signatory will not be accepted unless all of the existing signatories agree to accept him. As you can easily see, there are financial implications here."

Of course there were. As things stood at the time, the signatory teams to the Concorde Agreement would share, eight ways, a fixed percentage of the gross television revenue. This money was payable whether or not the commercial rights holder – in this case Bernie Ecclestone – made a profit or a loss on the overall operation of the various television coverage contracts through his FOCA TV organisa-

Above: Future multi-millionaire and Formula 1 commercial rights holder Bernie Ecclestone in action at the wheel. It is 1951, he's climbing Paddock Bend at Brands Hatch and he is just 20 years old. The preparation of his Formula 3 Cooper-Norton is immaculate, a portent of things to come. (LAT)

Left: Twenty three years later and Ecclestone is the sharp-suited businessman, owner of the Brabham Formula 1 team and starting out on his journey to public fame and fortune. (Author's collection)

Above: International motor racing had still to develop its
current well-polished professional gloss in the late 1960s as this impromptu
shot of the grandly titled London Racing Team's transporter tends to
suggest. Mosley (far right) acknowledges that the state of his jeans would
probably debar him from the F1 Paddock Club in 2003. His team-mate Chris
Lambert (with glasses) was killed at Zandvoort later in 1968, introducing
Mosley first-hand to motor racing's potentially tragic dimension. (LAT)

Above: Ecclestone (left) ran a pair of Formula 2 Lotus 69s under the Jochen Rindt Racing banner after Rindt himself was killed at Monza in 1970. Here he is in the pits at Bogota, Colombia, together with the promising young Italian driver Enzo Corti (with briefcase) and the legendary Graham Hill. Corti was killed a few months later in an Italian road accident. (LAT)

Below: Max Mosley tries the cockpit of his Formula 2 Brabham BT23C for size prior to embarking on his first serious season of international racing in 1968. (LAT)

Above: Enzo Ferrari was in many ways responsible for shaping the whole development of contemporary F1 racing in the sense that Ecclestone and Mosley quickly realised that the sport was nothing without the famous Italian racing team. Here the patriarchal figure addresses a media conference for visiting British press representatives at Maranello in 1986, two years before his death. He is flanked by his son Piero (right) and Marco Piccinini, his one-time team manager and a key behind-the-scenes player in the sport. (Author's collection)

Right: Ecclestone in quiet conference with Jackie Oliver, former team principal of the Arrows Formula 1 squad. Oliver sold out to entrepreneur Tom Walkinshaw in the mid-1990s, but the team was eventually overwhelmed by financial problems and went out of business at the end of 2002. (Author's collection)

Far right: Frank Williams back in the early 1970s when his team sometimes seemed to survive on thin air, yet always pulled through. Nobody needs to tell Williams how hard the F1 business can be. (LAT)

Above: When the world was young. From left, then McLaren team principal Teddy Mayer, Bernie Ecclestone, Max Mosley, Nina Rindt, widow of Jochen, and Debbie Rees, wife of Arrows director Alan Rees, in the pit lane at Paul Ricard during the 1976 French Grand Prix. (LAT)

Above: The colourful and rumbustious Jean-Marie Balestre marshalled the
FIA forces against the teams in the early 1980s. He was succeeded in 1991
as FIA president by Max Mosley who was fighting a similar battle – albeit
over different issues – by the start of the following decade. (LAT)

Right: Ferrari may be the most important team,
but great drivers such as Ayrton Senna and
Michael Schumacher are still the key factors in
attracting spectators – which is why the Drivers'
World Championship continues to be more
important than the Constructors' title. (LAT)

Above: The crown of Formula 1 is red. Eddie Irvine at the wheel of a Ferrari F300 during the Italian team's 600th race, the 1998 Belgian Grand Prix at Spa. The value to F1 of this remarkable racing team attracts extra attention - and corresponding extra payments. (Author's collection)

Above: Ecclestone as an F1 team principal. Watching over Carlos Pace's Brabham-Alfa Romeo BT45 in the pit lane at Brands Hatch, 1976 British Grand Prix. (LAT)

Above: Drivers' meeting prior to the 1977 South African Grand Prix at Kyalami with Ken Tyrrell (foreground) lecturing the troops. The drivers' influence as a powerbase within the Formula 1 business has ebbed and flowed over the years, largely dependent on the motivation of the leading lights at any given time. (LAT)

Right: Poignant moment. Jochen Rindt puts his helmet on for the last time prior to climbing into his Lotus 72 during final qualifying for the 1970 Italian Grand Prix at Monza. Within a few minutes Bernie Ecclestone's close friend and colleague would be dead, killed in a 170mph accident. Three decades later, with the advent of better-built cars and safer circuits – in part the legacy of sterling efforts by Bernie and Max Mosley – he would probably have walked away from a similar accident. (LAT)

Above: FIA president Max Mosley is strapped into the two-seater
McLaren-Mercedes MP4-98T before Martin Brundle drives him round
Silverstone during the 1999 British Grand Prix meeting. (LAT)

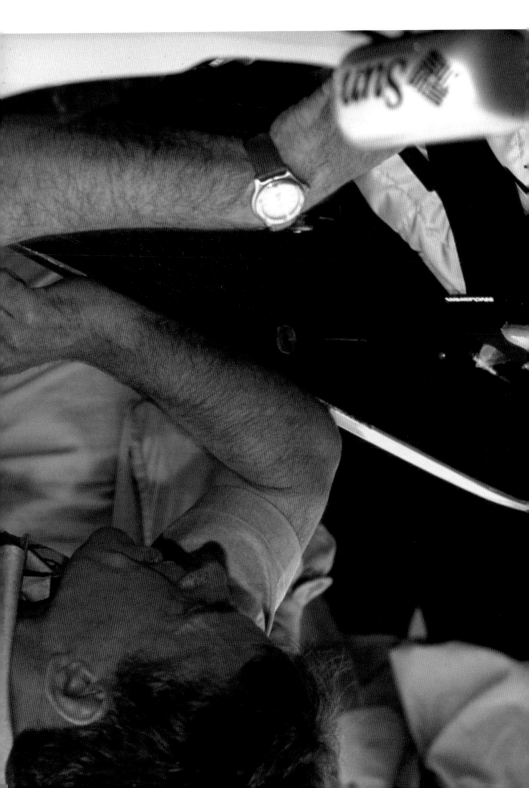

Above: The author (left) gets it first-hand from Bernie Ecclestone. Martin Whitaker, then Ford's competitions chief, and journalist Maurice Hamilton look on with suitably sceptical expressions on their faces. (LAT)

Left: Max Mosley looks unimpressed as McLaren boss Ron Dennis attempts to make a point. The two men have frequently clashed during the past few years over the question of how Formula 1 should be ruled and administered. (LAT)

Above: The allure of the Grand Prix business regularly brings out the A-list celebrities. Here Ecclestone escorts Jerry Hall and Mick Jagger on a visit to the Williams team's garage, with Frank in the foreground. (LAT)

Above: Master of all he surveys. Ecclestone arrives at Jerez during the 1997 European Grand Prix meeting, landing on the circuit just beyond the pits in his Jet Ranger helicopter. (LAT)

Right: The fruits of his labours. Bernie Ecclestone emerges from his own Learjet at the Spa airfield prior to the 2002 Belgian Grand Prix. He will be chauffeured to the circuit in the Mercedes S-class limousine in the foreground while his colleagues and paraphernalia will follow in the people carrier.

Above: Ecclestone with Piero Ferrari who retains a 10 per cent shareholding in the car company made famous by his father's efforts. Bernie has been shrewd enough to recognise Ferrari's huge contribution to the credibility of the F1 World Championship and ensures that the Italian company receives extra income from the commercial rights pot in acknowledgement of its unique status. (LAT)

Above: Frank Williams has been one of the stalwart supporters of the Formula
1 business for the past three decades. (LAT)

Above & left: Todt's organisational abilities and capacity to motivate the Maranello F1 workforce have become the stuff of legend. Former Ferrari driver Eddie Irvine thinks the ascetic Frenchman is the only man who could take over the command of the F1 business from Bernie Ecclestone. (LAT)

Above: Gianni Agnelli was always the symbolic driving force behind Ferrari within the Fiat industrial empire. He had saved Ferrari from oblivion in 1969 when he masterminded Fiat's rescue of the struggling sports car maker. (LAT)

Right: Balestre was a high-profile character with a shrewd sense of self-promotion. Here he is on the rostrum after the 1985 Dutch Grand Prix at Zandvoort together with winner Niki Lauda, second placeman Alain Prost (left) and Ayrton Senna. (LAT)

Above: The late Gianni Agnelli at a Ferrari function at Maranello; his attendance at these gatherings always created huge attention and interest. (LAT)

Right: Jean Todt with his boss and patron Luca di Montezemolo. Their joint contributions to Ferrari fortunes are unquestionably unmatched by any individuals since the death of company founder Enzo Ferrari in 1988. (LAT)

Above: Former rally ace Ove Andersson took charge of the Toyota F1 programme from its inauguration in 2001, having presided over the Japanese car maker's competitions programmes for more than two decades. (LAT)

Right: Jackie Stewart was not only a triple world champion who worked tirelessly to improve the sport's safety standards, but he and his son Paul also ran a successful Grand Prix team in the 1990s and Jackie has subsequently fought tenaciously to further the interests of the British Grand Prix in his role as president of the British Racing Drivers' Club. (LAT)

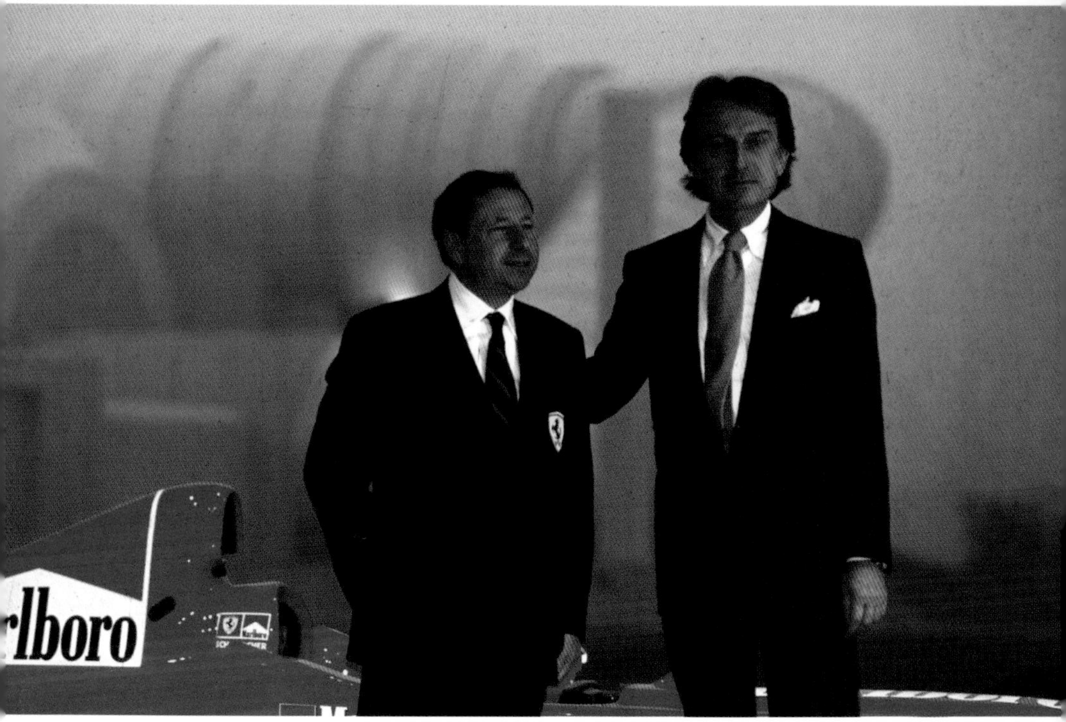
rlboro

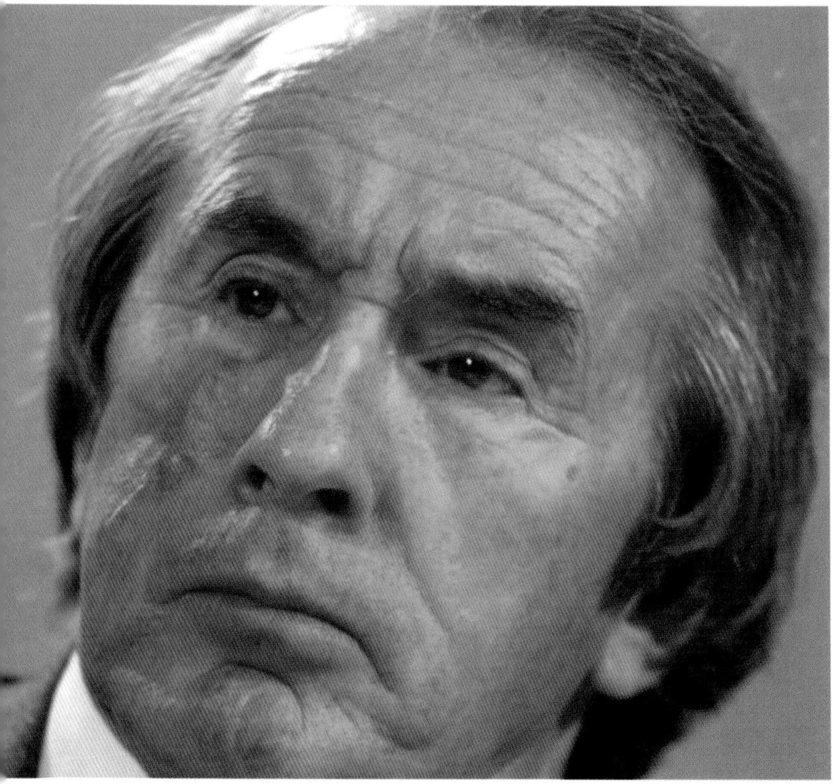

Above: Some of the most exclusive real estate in the world forms the circuit
on which the Monaco Grand Prix takes place. During race week in particular,
the fairy-tale principality is wall-to-wall with multi-million dollar yachts. (LAT)

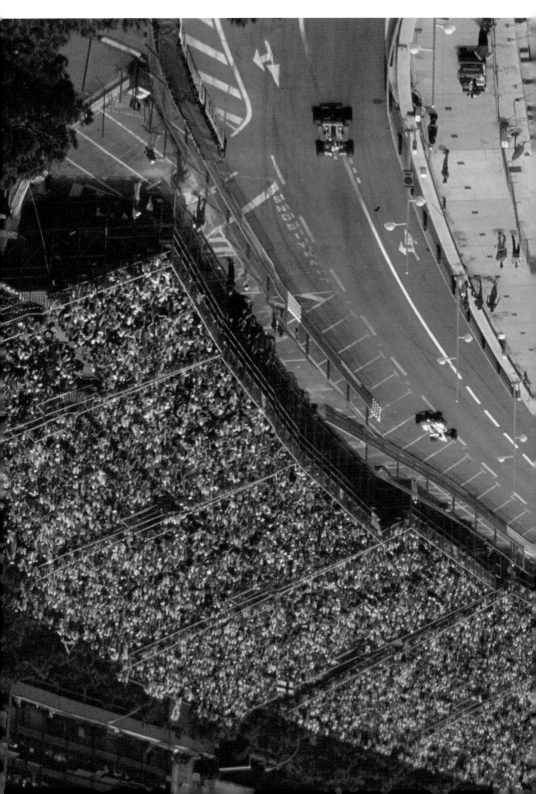

Above: Ferrari's dream team. From left, engine chief Paolo Martinelli, sporting director Jean Todt, Michael Schumacher and company president Luca di Montezemolo. (LAT)

Right: Michael Schumacher and Montezemolo. Luca's achievements in consolidating the health and expansion of the Ferrari empire are now legend. (LAT)

Below: Eddie Jordan has been one of the more colourful F1 team principals over the past decade, but his team has struggled to make ends meet over the past couple of seasons. (LAT)

Above: Peter Sauber owns and operates his F1 team in a modest and self-effacing way which reflects his own controlled, conservative style and manners. (LAT)

Left: F1's wealth cascades down the generations. Here Jenson Button relaxes on his yacht. (LAT)

Above: Such is the cosmopolitan attraction of F1 that even members of the royal family are drawn into its orbit. Here Princess Diana joins winner Damon Hill on the winner's rostrum at Silverstone after the 1994 British Grand Prix. (LAT)

Above: McLaren chairman Ron Dennis and DaimlerChrysler board member
Jurgen Hubbert raise a glass to their successful collaboration over the years.
Hubbert is also a leading light within the GPWC ranks and has become a
target for subtle criticism from the FIA as a result. (LAT)

Right: Even world
champions have to
check in and check out.
Here former
title-holder Mika
Hakkinen swipes his
card to gain access to
the F1 paddock. (LAT)

Above: David Richards became team principal of the BAR-Honda F1 team at the end of 2001 and is also commercial rights holder for the World Rally Championship as well as boss of the Prodrive organisation which prepares the works WRC Subarus. (LAT)

Overleaf: A public image of Formula 1 for the New Millennium. (LAT)

tion and associated subsidiaries.

The eight teams that had signed the Concorde Agreement eventually allowed the other three back into the fold after some discreet arm-twisting by Ecclestone and Mosley. For F1's *bruderbond*, ultimately it would be one for all and all for one.

08: CLASH OF INTERESTS? DID BERNIE FAVOUR HIS OWN TEAM?

"If you and I went into business together to purchase Marks &
Spencer, we wouldn't rename it Ecclestone & Henry, would we?"

Bernie's logic was unanswerable. I'd been interviewing him for
Motoring News in the late 1970s and that was his reply to my question as to why his F1 team still carried the name of its founder, Sir
Jack Brabham. In that respect, he was happily devoid of any ego. Not
that Ecclestone-BMW tripped off the tongue particularly smoothly, of
course.

Bernie purchased the Brabham team in 1971 and owned it for
18 years, during which time it won two World Championships in
1981 and '83. But did he abuse his position as a team principal? And
why when Piquet's Brabham-BMW was found to be using illegal fuel
in the 1983 South African GP – the race that clinched him his second
title for Brabham – was the whole matter apparently swept under
the carpet?

Ecclestone sold the Brabham team in the late 1980s, so these
episodes have now slipped into a rather charming historic perspective

as part of F1 folklore. There are even ex-Brabham personnel who now contend, over 20 years later that, yes, Brabham did run qualifying cars which were under the minimum weight limit. Illegal cars?

Ecclestone's critics at this time accused him of running with the hare and hunting with the hounds. The Brabham team, they said, always had advanced notice of regulation changes and were therefore in the pound seats when it came to anticipating which technical direction to take. In fact the evidence is quite to the contrary.

The fact that the 1.5-litre turbocharged Renault F1 challengers in the late 1970s were even allowed to race demonstrated the motor racing fraternity's ability to convince itself that black was white.

One Brabham old hand who continued rising through the ranks of the influential after Ecclestone sold the team was Charlie Whiting, now race director and safety delegate for the FIA and the man charged with implementing the governing body's F1 rule book. He went to work with Ecclestone in 1978 after a stint with the Hesketh team and has very vivid memories of his spell there.

"I'd prepared a Surtees TS19, for the British National Group 8 Shellsport Championship, which was owned by my brother Nick and driven by Divina Galica in 1977," he recalled. "Then Divina went to Hesketh for the first few Grands Prix the following year and I made the switch with her.

"But that didn't work out as neither she nor the car was really quick enough, so she was replaced by Eddie Cheever in South Africa and then Derek Daly drove it briefly in the Silverstone International Trophy. Then later that year I went to Brabham. My first race was the '78 fan car win in Sweden with Niki Lauda.

"I first met Bernie on the first day I started down at his factory in Chessington. I was just looking at the fan car for the first time and Bernie walked in. And of course he's always been 'Bernie.' We always knew him as Bernie, never Mr. Ecclestone.

"Working at Brabham was a bit special. But of course a lot of that came from working with Gordon Murray. In his design heyday, he was the catalyst; he was a little bit extrovert, both in his designs and behaviour, and we took our lead to some extent from him.

"But basically everyone had fun. We were almost encouraged to have fun."

So did Bernie let them get on with it? Or was he an interventionist manager? "Oh God yes," said Whiting. "He could be an interfering bastard. He was always standing on the pit wall with a couple of stopwatches he didn't know how to work. Then he would lose track, mutter 'fucking stopwatches' and thrown them down. But, yes, he did like to be involved."

In particular, Whiting recalled the 1987 San Marino Grand Prix when Riccardo Patrese was running second in the Brabham BT56 "which was pretty good for a Brabham in those days. He needed new tyres, but Bernie wouldn't let him stop.

"Then his team-mate Andrea de Cesaris was getting frantic: 'I wanna come in, I wanna come in.' And Bernie was standing on the pit wall yelling: 'No, stay out, stay out.' And I'm going: 'Bernie, for Christ's sake, he's got to stop for tyres. They're screwed.' In the meantime Andrea was getting more and more emotional. Eventually he came in for tyres with about five or six laps to go, I think, went straight back out again and immediately crashed the car because he was so stressed out by it all.

"So I think Bernie perhaps got a little more deeply involved than he should have done, but at the end of the day it was his bat, his ball and he wanted to play the game exactly as he saw it."

So has Bernie mellowed? "No, I think he's pretty much the same as he always was," said Whiting. "He still feels pretty passionate about the sport and can get pretty impatient with one or two of the leading players. He's the one who made them all rich, and these days he's not averse to reminding them of that in a pretty direct fashion."

Ecclestone took care to look after his staff when the Brabham team was sold.

"Do you want to stay with me?" he asked many of them. "I don't know what you're going to be doing, but it will be something." Those who stayed on included Whiting, his former team manager Herbie Blash, one of the very longest-serving members of the entire F1 community who started as a junior mechanic on Rob Walker's Lotus 49 back in 1968 and is now assistant race director at the Grands Prix, and Eddie Baker and Allan Woollard who work with Ecclestone's TV and management company. They've certainly been in for the long haul. While he could be a handful to deal with, his influence in the F1 business made life for the workers much more bearable.

Look at any paddock photograph in the 1950s and '60s. Gravel and dirt everywhere, haphazard layout, transporters varying from state-of-the-art equipment to poorly converted trucks. There was no real rhyme or reason to anything.

Bob Dance, who was chief mechanic with Brabham up until 1976, once told me he believed that Bernie's meticulous approach improved all the working conditions away from home beyond belief.

"Bernie was responsible for the enormous improvement in mechanics' working conditions during the 1980s," he said. "He was responsible for the nice pit garages, the neat and tidy organised paddock layouts. It was a reflection of his mentality, perhaps. Everything just so. He was always *very* particular."

While Ecclestone gave Murray a free hand with design, his determination to seek out a rare competitive advantage sometimes handicapped the Brabham team. For the 1976 season he cut a deal to use Alfa Romeo's 12-cylinder boxer engine. Not only was it available as a works deal, therefore eliminating the need to purchase engines from Cosworth, but it offered the advantage of more power. The idea was that it could go head-to-head with the all-conquering Ferrari flat-12s which were ruling the F1 roost at the time. That was the theory, anyway.

I remember being very impressed when I visited the Brabham F1 factory in 1975 to find a fax machine – then rather quaintly termed a "telecopier" – in Gordon's design office. This proved invaluable as the lanky, laid-back engineer endeavoured to work out how best to install the new flat-12 engine in the Brabham BT45.

The telecopier was invaluable because, as Gordon quickly discovered to his alarm, no two Alfa Romeo engines were *exactly* the same.

"Can you imagine that?" mused a somewhat bewildered Murray. "The engine mountings would vary by up to about half an inch, one from another. Mountings were different, because they'd perhaps skimmed the cylinder heads or re-machined the castings, or whatever. Oh yes, and the exhaust pipes always seemed to be pointing in different directions. Eventually we got the hang of it, but it was bloody difficult, I'll tell you."

The flat-12 Alfa Romeo was extremely difficult to install and cool, so although the 1977 Brabham BT45 proved a competitive machine, its development potential was extremely limited. Murray therefore decided to revert to his triangular monocoque chassis theme in 1978, the all-new BT46 featuring a highly imaginative system of "surface cooling".

This concept involved the engine water and oil being cooled by passing through a system of two water surface heat-exchangers and two oil surface heat-exchangers mounted within the monocoque structure. The liquid to be cooled flowed through a double-skinned channel which formed the outer wall and then through another special, finned outer surface which was licked by the airstream.

Niki Lauda was signed up to drive the new machine amidst a fanfare of media attention for the 1978 season. The trouble was, it just did not work. There were all sorts of installation problems with the heat-exchangers – and the BT46's water temperature rocketed off the clock when it was first tested at Donington Park. In January, in the depths of an English winter. It was not even worth daring to think what it might do in Buenos Aires or Brazil.

What Murray now had in mind to rectify the situation was dramatic in the extreme. In conditions of great secrecy, he decided that the best way to cool the car was to fit a large water radiator on top of the flat-12 Alfa engine – and then use a gearbox-driven fan to suck out all the air from beneath the car.

Thus was the Brabham "fan car" born. It stuck to the road like glue, gave Niki Lauda a massive performance advantage which enabled him to dominate the 1978 Swedish Grand Prix – and sent all the rival teams searching for their rule books.

Over that race weekend, a total of five teams protested the Brabham fan car's ineligibility, claiming that the *primary* reason for the development was to enhance the aerodynamics. If true, that was banned specifically by the rules. Ecclestone backed Murray's assertion that its *primary* purpose was to cool the engine. "Disconnect the fan and the engine overheats," said Gordon.

Lotus and Tyrrell immediately protested about the BT46B after its win, but the race stewards diplomatically ducked the issue and referred the matter to the CSI. Initially a compromise deal was proposed whereby Brabham could use the car for the next three races, after which they would withdraw it from competition.

Instead, the CSI banned such systems with immediate effect and, even before they did, Bernie decided to withdraw it anyway. He was shrewd enough not to rock the F1 team's sense of solidarity too hard. It was more important in his mind to keep the teams together as a cohesive entity rather than gain a short-term advantage for his own team.

Yet during the early 1980s, as Ferrari and Renault gradually began to get into the competitive swing of things with their turbocharged F1 cars, so the British-based teams, aligned with FOCA, began to worry that they might be hard pressed to win many races in the foreseeable future.

Most of these teams relied on Cosworth V8 engines developing around 480 horsepower, but this was nowhere near enough to match the turbos which had around 100 horsepower more. Resolving the problem involved the innovative British teams sitting down and carefully working out a clever ruse by which they could redress the balance of power. Quite literally.

For many years it had been the accepted practice to top up oil and water levels before cars were submitted for post-race scrutineering, thereby bringing them back up to their regulation weight by replenishing these liquids to "normal" level. Now the Cosworth-engined teams were thinking about a variation on that theme.

Lotus, Brabham, McLaren and the others all decided to fit their cars with reservoirs to carry water for brake-cooling purposes. These were filled up at the start of the race and, claimed the teams, the water was then used to cool air entering the brake ducts with the result that it was all consumed by the end of the race. Then the containers were re-filled, the cars scrutineered and they would make the minimum weight limit as required.

However, many people suspected that the entire contents of the water containers were dumped at the first corner. A cynical view, perhaps. In fact, the truth was even more convoluted. In many cases – some would say most – the water bottles were never filled in the first place. Therefore the Cosworth-engined runners were effectively running against the turbos to a separate – much lower – minimum weight limit. Or, to put it bluntly, they were running *beneath* the minimum weight limit in an effort to make up for their lack of horsepower.

This issue was first highlighted at the 1981 Monaco Grand Prix where Piquet's Brabham BT49C qualified on pole position just ahead of the mercurial Gilles Villeneuve's Ferrari 126CK, a very much heavier car.

The much-vexed question of underweight racing cars was now firmly in the spotlight. Most F1 insiders moderated their criticism of Ecclestone and the Brabham team, but Jacques Laffite grasped the nettle in an interview carried by the French sporting newspaper *L'Equipe*.

"Piquet has two cars, one ultra-light, which he uses in practice, and then his race car which is to normal weight," he claimed. "A regular Brabham is already on the weight limit. Good for them. But the practice car has carbon-fibre brake discs which save 12 kilos, and I'm told that the car also has a tiny fuel tank, much lighter than the normal one.

"The car should be weighed as soon as Piquet stops, before the mechanics can touch it. But no, no one will do anything, because it's a Brabham, owned by Ecclestone. Nobody can touch him. Everybody is frightened of him."

Twenty years later Patrick Head, the Williams technical director, would recall with wry amusement how Charlie Whiting, then chief mechanic at Brabham, would taunt the Williams crew by waving the lightweight wings at them from just along the pit lane. Today Whiting, of course, is another poacher turned gamekeeper in the role of F1 race director. And respected with it.

Under these circumstances, it was perhaps ironic that Nelson Piquet drove to his first World Championship in 1981 at the wheel of the Ecclestone-owned Brabham BT49. In those days Ecclestone left the day-to-day running of the Brabham team to his trusted lieutenants, most notably chief designer Gordon Murray, while he tried to field all the contentious issues in the battle with the FISA.

At the time, these individual scuffles seemed sufficiently serious to be taken at face value. Yet it was the sub-text to the disputes, several of which erupted over different seemingly individual issues over a period of three seasons, which one realises, with hindsight, was much more important.

Ecclestone had shrewdly realised the potential for growth of televised sports and was determined that he and the teams would have their share of this particular goose, which seemed set to continue to lay golden eggs into the distant future. Bernie was right on target and would become one of the richest men in Britain as a result of that perspicacity.

As recounted in detail elsewhere in this volume, in 1980 the preliminary skirmish between FOCA and FISA had come to a head over a sanctioning dispute at the Spanish Grand Prix

Alan Jones won the race for Williams, but the result was not allowed to count for the World Championship. The same happened at the following year's South African Grand Prix. FOCA had laid its own plans to combat the sliding-skirt ban by taunting FISA with threats of a breakaway world championship run by the "World Federation of Motor Sports" which would run its contest for cars still using these aerodynamic appendages.

In fact, the World Federation of Motor Sports never existed and its rather grand looking statutes, circulated in a document at the time, were drafted by Ecclestone's legal advisor and collaborator Max Mosley and committed to print by Ian Phillips, today director of business development for the Jordan team. So, having played this game themselves, it is perhaps easy to understand why Ecclestone and Mosley are so scathing about the credibility of the planned GPWC series.

FOCA lost its second confrontation with FISA. Running on ragtag used tyres – because the tyre companies did not dare risk the FIA's wrath by supplying new rubber – the F1 teams managed to produce some semblance of a motor race at Kyalami to open the 1981 season. But again, Carlos Reutemann's victory in a Williams was not permitted to stand.

Eventually, just prior to the Long Beach Grand Prix, FISA and FOCA reached a rapprochement with the signing of the Concorde Agreement, which laid out the procedures whereby regulations could be changed and, while acknowledging FISA's role as the sporting power, effectively left the financial control in the hands of the constructors.

Thus the 1981 season continued without fixed skirts. But the whole Championship programme was blighted by the need to build ridiculously complicated suspension systems to enable the competing cars to conform to a new FISA rule demanding a 6cm ground clearance when they were checked in the pits while still running as close to the ground as possible while out on the circuit.

Brabham's Gordon Murray and his colleague David North came

up with the best way round the rule. They devised with a system of soft air springs which the aerodynamic load compressed as the speed built up, dropping the BT49C contender down to a ground-effect stance. As the speed dropped away again when the car arrived in the pit lane, so it rose on its suspension to clear the 6cm requirement.

The system worked brilliantly at Buenos Aires where Piquet ran away with the Argentine Grand Prix, the third race of the title chase, and the rest of the field erupted in fury. Rivals objected on the basis that, in their view, the Brabhams were running flexible skirts – not sliding skirts – and, in the view of the Williams team, for one, this was not legal.

This was another example of Ecclestone supposedly gaining a leg-up over his rivals due to his pre-eminent position within the sport. The Williams team in particular, whose car driven by Carlos Reutemann had been roundly beaten into second place in Argentina, were left fuming by what they clearly regarded as the Brabham team's over-liberal interpretation of the rules. But the result was allowed to stand.

Murray simply shrugged them aside, accusing his rivals of being bad losers, but then the FISA issued a rule clarification on the subject and the whole issue of the complex Brabham suspension system became irrelevant when several of the cars arrived for the Belgian Grand Prix fitted with suspension lowering switches in the cockpit. The FISA officials figuratively threw up their hands in horror and that was effectively the end of that.

By the start of the 1982 season it was clear that even the British, FOCA-aligned teams would need to secure a supply of turbocharged engines if they were to remain competitive. For Ecclestone, this meant cutting a deal with BMW for the use of its prodigiously powerful, production-based four-cylinder 1.5-litre turbo. The engine had first run on the test bed in 1980 and been tested in a Brabham chassis in 1981, long before it was raced.

In today's F1 environment the car manufacturers have considerable clout and influence, but back in 1982 when BMW tried strong-arm tactics, attempting to bully Ecclestone into running the underdeveloped BMW engines rather than the existing Cosworth-propelled Brabhams, they got nowhere fast.

Ecclestone was concerned that the BMW engine was insufficiently reliable, but BMW's patience snapped after the British teams – including Brabham – boycotted the 1982 San Marino Grand Prix as an ongoing element of their battle with the FIA over the control of F1's commercial rights.

Immediately afterwards BMW issued a statement threatening to terminate its engine supply deal with Ecclestone unless Nelson Piquet and Riccardo Patrese drove their Brabham-BMWs in the next race, the Belgian Grand Prix. The cars had made their debut in the South African GP at the start of the season, where the high altitude Kyalami circuit gave the turbos a performance edge, but then the team had back-tracked to its Cosworth-engined machines for the Brazilian race.

The statement added: "Should this requirement not be met by Mr Ecclestone, BMW will terminate its co-operation with Brabham."

In fact, the Brabham-BMWs subsequently raced with increasing competitiveness over the balance of the season. Gordon Murray's strategic ingenuity also re-introduced pit stops for refuelling into the F1 equation as private tests confirmed that – in theory at least – it was better for these very powerful cars to start races on light fuel loads which would enable them to build up a sizeable lead before coming into the pits to top up their tanks. Over a race distance, it looked like being the quickest route to victory.

Meanwhile, on the political scene, a major debate was raging as to what should be done about the F1 technical regulations for 1983. The FOCA teams had honed their development of under-car aerodynamics to a very sophisticated level and were anxious that this performance advantage should not be eroded.

By the same token, the governing body was adamant that

ground-effect aerodynamics should be ruled out for 1983. That was largely because the FISA was being lobbied by Ferrari, Renault and Alfa Romeo, all of which had powerful engines at their disposal but lacked chassis technology on anything like the level enjoyed by the British teams.

FISA also claimed that lap speeds were spiralling out of control. After all, Piquet's pole position time for the Austrian Grand Prix at the super-fast Osterreichring circuit had topped an average speed of 151mph. In a Brabham-BMW turbo.

Gordon Murray was now about to discover that working for the most powerful individual in Formula 1 did not always work out to the Brabham team's advantage. What followed proved that Ecclestone did not have prior knowledge of any technical rule change which could give Murray and his design team a head start in their labours.

Notwithstanding the prevailing trend of opinion against ground effect, Bernie remained totally convinced that it would not be out-lawed for 1983. Consequently, when Murray asked for guidance, he received the green light to build a compact little ground-effect Brabham – the BT51 – which was fitted with a very small fuel tank to take advantage of the refuelling possibilities.

"The whole transmission was designed, the patterns were under-way – and then the FISA banned ground effect," recalled Murray. "Bernie had said 'don't worry, don't worry' as he sought to reassure me over the previous months. Then one day he came in and said 'worry.' And we had to scrap everything we'd done and start all over again."

A little over a year later, Nelson Piquet clinched the 1983 World Championship with a third place finish in the South African Grand Prix at Johannesburg's Kyalami circuit. In doing so, he defeated the much-touted Renault turbo of his key rival Alain Prost – and the French driver paid for this failure by being sacked from his job, a stu-pid and ill-considered decision by a racing team which clearly could not understand that its own technical lack of competitiveness lost it the battle with Brabham-BMW.

Or was there more to it than that? In the aftermath of this success, BMW found itself on the receiving end of a most unpalatable postscript when it was suggested that the fuel employed in the Brabhams had exceeded the 102RON octane rating that was permitted under the regulations.

This little nugget of information was published, admittedly without any comment, by a rival fuel company after independent tests on samples of BMW fuel had indicated a problem after the Kyalami race. But no action was ever taken and BMW's then competitions manager, Dieter Stappert, fiercely rebutted any suggestion that the fuel could have been illegal, citing the exhaustive checking procedures which every batch was subjected to prior to being released for competitive use.

Yet, to this day, nobody has offered a definitive and satisfactory explanation of this apparent discrepancy. Twenty years later when the episode is discussed, it prompts raised eyebrows. Was it an innocent error?

Or did the Ecclestone-owned Brabhams clinch the 1983 World Championship illegally? It is unlikely that a definitive verdict will ever be reached.

09: POACHERS TURNED GAMEKEEPERS

The route by which Ecclestone and Mosley took control of the Formula 1 business was not simply one which related directly to commercial interests or sporting control. There were hard technical justifications by which the predominantly British FOCA-aligned teams lined up behind Ecclestone in the early 1980s. In short, those teams felt that the FIA was showing partiality against them in favouring the "Grandees", the motor industry-backed teams which were represented by Ferrari, Renault and Alfa Romeo.

The trouble had started in 1977 when the first Renault V6 turbo had taken to the tracks at the British Grand Prix. This unreliable newcomer was not taken seriously. The British teams regarded turbocharging as an unnecessarily over-complex means of interpreting a rule that had remained on the F1 statute book for more than a decade simply because nobody had bothered to delete it.

Between 1949 and '51 the F1 rules were governed by regulations which provided for 1.5-litre supercharged or 4.5-litre non-supercharged engines. In reality, such notional equivalency was just plucked from the sky. There was no totally reliable method of predicting which would produce the most power, let alone which equation of relative cylinder capacity would provide some semblance of parity between the two.

There were various changes to the equivalency rule in subsequent years, though there were no serious attempts to use supercharging, until in 1966 the rule was set at 1.5-litres "with compressor" or at 3-litres naturally aspirated – without compressor. The rule makers did not think to differentiate between supercharging or turbocharging as methods of compression, though there were substantial differences.

The new rule was basically a fall-back position in case there developed, as was feared, a grave shortage of 3-litre racing engines at the start of the new formula, which might jeopardise the future of F1.

The concept of turbocharging was originally applied by the aviation industry as a method of sustaining intake manifold pressure at altitude on piston-engined aircraft. At higher altitudes the rate at which air can be introduced into a combustion chamber to mix with incoming fuel is obviously reduced by the lower barometric pressure.

At sea level, air density is 1-bar – around 14 pounds per square inch. But at 3000 feet, the density of the air drops to 0.85-bar. Thus a piston-engined aircraft loses performance the higher it flies, in the same way that a car engine loses performances when it is being operated at high altitude.

The great advantage of turbocharging over supercharging is that the former consumes little in the way of power simply to drive itself. A supercharger, powered by gearing taken off the engine, needed up to 70bhp just to drive it, before adding any power. A turbocharger is driven by the exhaust gases, producing extra power more or less "free", although it produces back pressure against which the pistons have to fight on the exhaust stroke.

The FIA had decided that 1.5-litre turbocharged engines equated to the breed of 3-litre naturally aspirated units being used by the majority of the field. In truth, and as many F1 engine designers would later make the point, it was virtually impossible to accurately frame such comparisons between the performance of naturally aspirated and forced-induction engines.

In any event, there would turn out to be no shortage of 3-litre F1 engines. In particular, the advent of the Ford-financed Cosworth DFV V8 in 1967 would transform the entire commercial and sporting landscape of the F1 business.

It was the ultimate irony that the engine which enabled F1 to thrive and expand for well over a decade would eventually be eclipsed by one developed under rules which the DFV had originally been seen to make totally redundant.

One of the most vocal critics of the turbo in F1 was Keith Duckworth, the man behind the Cosworth-Ford DFV. In the late 1970s or early 1980s, if you wanted a really brisk argument in the pit lane, the easiest means of securing it was to ask Keith what he thought about the new generation of turbos. He did not approve, nor did he believe them to be legal.

The first seeds of a turbocharged F1 engine had been sown in the early 1970s, although not perhaps intentionally. Renault began its serious contemporary motor racing involvement in a low key fashion, starting with a 2-litre, four-cam V6 built round an iron cylinder block for the then-prestigious European 2-litre Sports Car Championship.

When the company decided to go into F1, it was not content simply to compete against the existing teams on the current rules. Renault wanted to showcase its technical excellence, deciding to build both chassis and engine, which only Ferrari did at that time, and to go up the audacious and unprecedented turbocharged route.

Renault reduced the stroke of the 2-litre V6 to bring the engine down to 1.5-litres, but it quickly became obvious that when this was turbocharged, there were serious shortcomings to be surmounted. From the drivers' standpoint, the most obvious was "turbo lag", which meant that there was a delay between the driver opening the throttle and the power chiming in. This would provide a major headache for pretty well all the turbo F1 teams over the next few years.

The F1 turbo era began with that tentative Renault V6 outing at Silverstone, but by 1982/83 it was absolutely into top gear with engines from Ferrari, BMW, Honda, Alfa Romeo and Hart all joining the French car maker which had started the trend. At its absolute zenith, this chapter of Grand Prix racing history spawned some of the most spectacular and powerful F1 cars of all time.

BMW's turbo eventually produced an estimated 1400bhp. "Estimate," said its designer Paul Rosche, "since our dynamometers back then didn't go beyond 1280bhp!"

Thereafter a progressive reduction in turbo boost pressure over the next two seasons produced a gentle, tactical retreat from the world of forced-induction Grand Prix cars. The final race of the turbocharged era was won by Alain Prost's McLaren-Honda MP4/4 at Adelaide at the end of the 1988 season.

Renault won the first race for a turbocharged engine in 1979, to its delight at its home French Grand Prix, but Jody Scheckter won the World Championship in the conventionally engined Ferrari. It was, however, a combination of Michelin radial rubber and bullet-proof r·liability which counted for more than the qualities of the 312T4 chassis or its engine.

More significant by far was the emergence of the Williams team in 1979 and the near collapse of both Lotus and McLaren. The Williams FW07 would develop the ground effect concept pioneered by Lotus to fresh levels of performance, its chassis being considerably stiffer than Chapman's car, which faded from the scene in 1979. The Williams did not make its race debut until the fifth round of the title chase, but Jones and team-mate Clay Regazzoni quickly indicated that it was a highly promising proposition. For the British Grand Prix, Jones would be the man to beat.

After an initial skirmish with Jabouille's Renault turbo, Jones stormed off into the distance only to be sidelined by a cracked water pump. That let Regazzoni through to achieve the historic distinction of the Williams team's first win. Jones won four more races in 1979 to end up third in the World Championship on 40 points, trailing new champion Scheckter (51 points net) and Gilles Villeneuve (47 net).

Now Williams and designer Patrick Head were on their way. In 1980, the FW07B, still equipped with full sliding skirts, emerged as the car of the year and carried Alan Jones to the World Championship. It is no coincidence that Williams had its own wind tunnel and recruited its own aerodynamicist during 1979, the highly respected Frank Dernie, and this helped them sustain their performance edge into the following year.

In 1980 Jones was joined by Argentine former Lotus driver Carlos Reutemann, who won the Monaco Grand Prix, and found himself locked in a head-to-head battle for the title with the young Brazilian driver Nelson Piquet who had emerged as a world-class contender at the wheel of the Gordon Murray-designed Brabham-Ford BT49 at the end of the previous year.

Ecclestone had decided to ditch the unreliable new Alfa Romeo V12 engines which had been developed for 1979 in an effort to make a ground-effect chassis design more feasible. Niki Lauda thought the new engines were awful and their inconsistent performance through the summer of 1979 contributed to his decision to quit.

The switch to Cosworth-Ford DFVs in time for the '79 Canadian Grand Prix was too late to retain Niki's interest and he walked away from F1 and the team mid-way through the first practice session. The Renault turbo took three victories in 1980 and the following year Ferrari also went turbo, joined in the new technology by Brian Hart, whose engine powered Toleman, the team later bought by Benetton.

Meanwhile, as Ron Dennis worked meticulously to estimate what sort of budget would be needed to launch an F1 team of their own, a convergence of well-timed circumstances gave an added fillip to his efforts. The McLaren team's deteriorating form since James

Hunt had won the Championship in 1976 had been a matter of some concern to Marlboro, its title sponsor.

As a result, Marlboro engineered an amalgamation between the team and Dennis's own Project 4 organisation which had gained its success in the second division formulae. McLaren chief Teddy Mayer's 85 per cent stake in the original Team McLaren now became 45 per cent of the new company, McLaren International, which sustained his position as the largest single shareholder. Yet it was the energy of Dennis and his Project 4 partner Creighton Brown, a former amateur racer and keen businessman, which began to transform the team's image.

On the engineering front, Dennis and designer John Barnard – another of the elite group of innovative F1 engineers – successfully concluded a deal with the US Hercules Aerospace company for the supply of carbon fibre composite panels which would be bonded together to form the chassis of the radical new McLaren MP4.

Happily, everything went to plan with John Watson scoring the team's first win at Silverstone in 1981 – with a DFV engine – after Rene Arnoux's Renault turbowilted with engine trouble. Five years had passed since John scored his sole previous F1 victory for the American Penske team in the 1976 Austrian Grand Prix and this latest success had not come a moment too soon.

For 1982, Dennis would hit the headlines by persuading Niki Lauda to come out of a retirement which had lasted two and a half years and, while the team would continue with Cosworth-Ford DFVs for the moment, the management began to lay plans for its own turbocharged engine. Dennis was ambitious and Barnard totally uncompromising when it came to engineering the cars, so it was unlikely that either of them would be satisfied with any of the existing turbos already on the Grand Prix scene.

Dennis eventually commissioned Porsche to build a bespoke V6 engine which would be funded by McLaren and carry the TAG brand name in acknowledgement of McLaren's prestige shareholder. But the new engine would not be ready to race until late in 1983 and, in the meantime, Dennis and McLaren would remain members of the Ecclestone-aligned, Cosworth V8 brigade.

The Ferrari switch to turbocharged engine technology in 1981 yielded two Grand Prix victories with the 126CK, as this first rough and ready turbocar was designated. Both were scored by Gilles Villeneuve, one through sheer driving brilliance at Monaco, the other by shrewd tactics and total consistency at the head of a jinking queue of cars during the Spanish Grand Prix at Jarama.

The trusty Renault EF1 was now developing around 540bhp at 11,5000rpm, and the Ferrari 126C had now been developed to produce around 20bhp more than its French counterpart. But the most exciting engine of all was being developed by BMW, although it would not be ready to race until the start of the 1982 season.

As Ferrari and Renault gradually began to get into the competitive swing of things with their turbocharged F1 cars, so the British-based teams, aligned with FOCA, began to worry that they might be hard pressed to win many races in the foreseeable future.

One symbolic illustration of their concern surrounded Colin Chapman's latest imaginative solution for chassis development, the Lotus 86 and 88 projects, both of which turned into a protracted saga in 1981.

After the Lotus 79 and its successor, the aerodynamically complex type 80, failed to sustain a competitive F1 pace in 1979, Colin Chapman's research and development department began to lay plans to redress the situation.

The way in which aerodynamic loadings had increased dramatically with the second generation of ground-effect machines preoccupied their thoughts and they turned to examining ways in which the aerodynamic forces could be isolated from the chassis itself.

Lotus's answer was the type 86 which was originally tested at the end of 1980 during the last season of the sliding-skirt rules. Wind tunnel testing had convinced Chapman's engineers that, instead of having separate sliding skirts moving up and down relative to the bodywork, it would be better to spring-mount the body structure on the wheel uprights, thereby transmitting the aerodynamic loadings directly to the suspension and tyres, while at the same time incorporating a conventionally sprung chassis riding free within the movable aerodynamic body.

This concept would at one and the same time stabilise the under-car aerodynamics and insulate the driver from the physical battering caused by the ultra-stiff suspension. Unfortunately FISA got wind of what was happening and issued a "rule clarification" making the point that any part of the car influencing its aerodynamic performance must be rigidly secured to the entirely sprung part of the car "and must remain immobile in relation to the sprung part of the car".

In Chapman's view this attitude undermined the two-year rule stability which was an essential element within the Concorde Agreement he had helped draft and then signed. He pressed on to produce a fixed-skirt version of the concept built round a carbon-fibre/Kevlar monocoque and dubbed the type 88. Unfortunately a succession of protests and unfavourable edicts from the governing body guaranteed the downfall of the "twin-chassis" Lotus before it ever raced.

The issue of cars running under the weight limit bubbled along through 1981 and then erupted again at the 1982 Brazilian Grand Prix. But this time it almost triggered another terminal split between FOCA and FISA.

Nelson Piquet's Brabham BT49D won the race ahead of Keke Rosberg's Williams FW07C with Alain Prost's Renault turbo RE30B finishing third. During the course of the race, Piquet's featherweight Brabham had hustled Gilles Villeneuve's heavier and less wieldy Ferrari turbo into a driving error and the Canadian spun off the circuit into a barrier.

However, the stewards of the Rio race were having none of the

FOCA teams' tactics. They disqualified Piquet and Rosberg, thereby handing the race to Prost's Renault. The Brabham and Williams teams appealed, but a Court of Appeal convened by FISA upheld the disqualification. In turn, the FOCA teams alleged that this disqualification constituted a change in the rules. For its part, the governing body retorted that, far from being a change in the rules, it was merely a clarification.

FOCA dramatically over-played its hand with a stubborn display of trades union-style muscle when it came to the San Marino Grand Prix at Imola. They boycotted this event, with the result that it was contested only by Ferrari, Renault, Osella, Toleman, ATS and the renegade Tyrrell team which, despite its alignment with FOCA, found itself obliged to take part on the insistence of its Italian sponsors.

In what was seen at the time as an effort to placate his furious FOCA colleagues, Tyrrell also used the San Marino GP weekend as an opportunity to fire the first volley in the next major argument. He lodged a formal protest against all turbocharged cars competing at this event on the basis that their engines included turbines and, since turbines were banned by the F1 regulations, these were effectively illegal secondary power units.

The race was won by Didier Pironi's Ferrari 126C2 after the Frenchman tricked his team-mate Gilles Villeneuve on the final lap. Pironi effectively gained his success against team orders and, 13 days later, Gilles was killed practising for the Belgian Grand Prix at Zolder. It was the start of a nightmare season for Ferrari which would see Pironi's career ended by horrendous leg injuries during practice for the German Grand Prix. It was also the season which effectively saw the FOCA teams cut and run into the turbo enclave. At the end of the day, they were in the racing business and winning races meant you had to go faster than the opposition. And in 1982, that meant having a turbocharged F1 engine.

Meanwhile, Bernie Ecclestone had very shrewdly been hedging his bets as far as the Brabham team was concerned. The team had tested a BMW four-cylinder turbocharged engine as long ago as the '81 British Grand Prix, where Piquet appeared with the BT50 prototype during practice, but the unit was not raced until the start of the following year.

Of course, after the 1981 season had been punctuated by arguments about the rules and technical controversies, it was ironic that 1982 kicked off with a major row involving the drivers, and that it overshadowed Brabham's conversion to the turbo engine.

Niki Lauda, returning to drive for McLaren, provided the catalyst for this unfortunate confrontation. While examining the paperwork which accompanied his FIA super-licence prior to the start of the season, he suddenly realised that the governing body had issued the licence in conjunction with a specific team. It was not, if you like, a "stand alone" licence issued individually to the Austrian.

The drivers quickly concluded that the FIA and the team owners had conspired to establish a restrictive cartel, leaving them as nothing more than pawns in a big-budget chess game. They threatened a strike unless things were changed and, partly at least, carried out their threat by missing the first practice session at Kyalami for the South African Grand Prix.

Eventually the strike was broken by an apparent compromise which did not prevent the FISA imposing fines on those who had transgressed. It was an unsatisfactory episode which did not reflect well on the drivers, but the significance of which was probably swamped by wider issues engulfing the sport at that time.

Through all this controversy, mechanical mayhem and off-track politicking, the feisty, extrovert Keke Rosberg picked his way through other people's debris to take the Championship at the wheel of the naturally aspirated Williams FW08. Rosberg, who joined Williams only at the start of the '82 season, drove his heart out from start to finish. Although he only won a single Grand Prix, it was certainly an unusual year in that no other driver won more than two races throughout.

Meanwhile, ground-effect aerodynamics were swept away for the 1983 season when the FISA decreed that all cars should have flat bottoms from the start of the year. More welcome was the news that there was to be stability of engine regulations through to the end of 1985, plus a reduction in minimum weight to 540kg and, from the start of 1984, plans to reduce fuel tankage from 250 to 220 litres.

Most immediately affected by this was Gordon Murray who had remained confident that there would be no changes to the rules affecting under-car aerodynamics for 1983 .

Encouraged by the obvious potential of the in-race refuelling stop, Murray decided to take this concept a step further for 1983 with a "half-tank" chassis, dubbed the BT51, complete with a radical new transmission which would was designed to get the best out of ground-effect aerodynamics. Suddenly, on that fateful day, 3 November 1982, Murray realised that the new car would have to be scrapped.

And so he started again. Brabham had to produce a totally new car to the new flat-bottomed rules and it had to be ready for the Brazilian Grand Prix on the following 13 March. That was the dead-line and there was absolutely no question of missing it.

It was ready in time. Piquet started as he meant to go on in 1983, storming to victory in the Brazilian Grand Prix at Rio with the new BT52 and keeping the car pretty well in play for the rest of the season. In-race refuelling would remain an integral component in F1 race strategy throughout the season, although it would be banned for 1984, and the Brabham mechanics came to be regarded as possibly the most accomplished performers in this respect. Nelson won his second title with the new car.

The turbo era was now in full swing and would be for the next five seasons. With Honda aligning itself with the Williams squad and the new TAG turbo blossoming into a force which would carry McLaren to three straight World Championships, the racing would be consistently compelling and absorbing.

More crucially, Ecclestone had nailed down the commercial side of the business for the benefit of the teams. The scene was set for F1's golden years.

Yet by the end of 1987 it had been decided that the turbo engines would be scrapped. The 1988 season was unique in that it allowed two different types of car to compete in the FIA Formula 1 World Championship, both qualifying equally for points in both the Drivers' and Constructors' title battles.

On the one hand, a team could opt to run under the 3.5-litre naturally aspirated rules to a 500kg minimum weight limit, a formula which would become obligatory.

On the other, it could opt for a final fling with the 1.5-litre turbos. Many people believed they did not have a chance, restricted as they were by a 2.5-bar boost limitation, a 150-litre fuel capacity maximum and a 540kg minimum weight limit.

One such individual was FISA president Jean-Marie Balestre who, speaking at a meeting at Estoril in late 1986 to announce this interim season, made one of those memorable remarks that could match anything a professional politician might utter in its capacity for being wide of the mark.

"I promise you, gentleman, in 1988, no way for the turbos," said Balestre. He would have been correct in that prediction had it not been for the McLaren-Hondas. They simply won 15 out of the season's 16 races. If they hadn't been there, the laurels would have been pretty evenly spread between naturally aspirated and turbocharged competition. But they were.

From here on the battle would be for revs. High-revving naturally aspirated engines would be the order of the day. But as Honda president Nobuhiko Kawamoto warned: "In a few years' time the turbos will look cheap compared with the naturally aspirated engines. Remember, boost is cheaper than revs."

Kawamoto was to be proved absolutely correct. At the very zenith of F1's achievement and popularity, the seeds for the economic downfall were being sown. Ten years down the road, they would have grown into an engine supply and cost crisis the like of which the sport could never have imagined in its wildest nightmares.

10: STRANGE BEDFELLOWS; F1'S NEW MILLIONAIRES

The team principals around the table at the Heathrow Hilton Hotel froze, almost unable to believe what they had heard.

"Don't you speak to David Richards like that," Max Mosley told Ron Dennis. "When the rest of us were busy building this business back in the 1970s, you were going bust in Formula 2."

The FIA president was seeking to admonish the McLaren team principal for intervening, in turn, to disagree with the BAR-Honda team principal David Richards. Yet Mosley had gone too far and allowed a touch of theatrical exaggeration to pepper his criticism – particularly when one considers that Richards was one of the newest kids on the F1 block.

Dennis had never gone bust. He had ceased trading with one of his F2 projects back in the 1970s and paid off all his creditors. But Max's interjection was another example of the crackling tension which existed between the two men. Frank Williams later whispered to Mosley that on this occasion he had gone too far. Max corrected himself.

By any standards they are a disparate group. At first glance they seem like a mildly dysfunctional family, bound together by circumstance and history. All different, with widely varying ambitions, barely concealed personal agendas, partisan loyalties and an eye for the main chance.

So you can see that the current generation of Formula 1 millionaire team principals represents a remarkable cross section of global sport's *arrivistes*. Add to them Mosley and Ecclestone and you have a sport which is governed and influenced by shifting alliances and clandestine groupings. To the uninformed outsider it may seem that the inmates are being allowed to run the asylum, but it is more complicated than that. A lot more complicated.

The upper echelons of the Formula 1 business are an a uneasy democracy based partly on mutual interest and partly on how one can harness a personal advantage. A real case of ask not what you can do for your colleague, but how you can manoeuvre him into the firing line. Thirty years ago Frank Williams gave thanks to the heavens when Ford loaned him a Zodiac saloon. Now he rides the heavens in a $28m Falcon 900 executive jet.

It is fair to say that his income and that of his F1 colleagues has easily outstripped the UK's retail price index since he first became involved in this most alluring and addictive of international sports.

If you met a group of F1 team owners over a dinner table for the first time, you would surely conclude that they are an unusual bunch. Dennis with his Howard Hughes-like obsession with cleanliness and detail; Williams, the ultimate petrol head; Flavio Briatore, running the Renault team, a shadowy figure from the fringes; Richards, the one-time rally co-driver who now owns a multi-million dollar engineering business as well as controlling the commercial rights to the World Rally Championship.

There is Peter Sauber, the ascetic and conservative Swiss, Paul Stoddart, the extrovert Australian owner of European Aviation whose passion for F1 led him to buy into the Minardi team. Plus former international rally star Ove Andersson looking after the interests of Toyota, ironically sitting at table with Jean Todt, now one of the sport's most powerful personalities in his role as Ferrari sporting director, but who 30 years ago was one of Andersson's rally co-drivers.

For his part, Ron Dennis is a focused technocrat. He began as a mechanic on Jochen Rindt's Cooper-Maserati at the age of 19 and was always more fascinated by motor racing's potential for engineering excellence than the cars themselves. Yet he is an utter professional, totally committed to success.

In 1981 Dennis, whose Project Four company had been steered into an amalgamation with the then-tottering McLaren squad thanks to the insistence of title sponsors Marlboro, targeted Williams sponsor TAG as a possible future partner to bankroll its new Porsche-made turbocharged engine.

"Ron was pretty quick on his feet," concedes Frank, "and he certainly did a very good sales job on Mansour Ojjeh. We were very unhappy about it at the time, but Ron was simply looking after his own interests in a competitive business." Ojjeh was the tri-lingual son of Akram Ojjeh, the founder of TAG – Techniques d'Avante Garde – whose interests had ranged from arms sales to brokering the sale of the transatlantic liner, *France*. TAG soon took a stake in the McLaren empire and currently controls a 30 per cent stake, equal to that of Ron Dennis.

Today the TAG McLaren group is a highly successful company which is 40 per cent owned by DaimlerChrysler.

Dennis had made a shrewd move which, at the time, looked like Williams's loss. McLaren duly developed their bespoke TAG turbo V6 and waltzed off with a hat-trick of World Championships in 1984-86, although Williams managed to sneak the Constructors' crown in the third year.

By then, of course, Frank and his technical chief Patrick Head had built an engine supply partnership with Honda which would buttress the making of Nigel Mansell's reputation and help Nelson

Piquet to a third World Championship in 1987.

Dennis makes no secret of his respect for his key rival. "Like ourselves, Williams is a *real* Grand Prix team with good vertical integration and a commitment to success," he said. "With the inevitable ups and downs that one experiences in F1, inevitably while I know Frank and Patrick well, I think our respective responsibilities have seen me grow a particularly strong friendship with Frank.

"Frank and I are fiercely competitive, but whilst I'd like to think we enjoy each other's company, it's really the trust, respect and integrity that we hold for each other which really matters."

For his part, Williams is the archetypal racing enthusiast, absolutely committed to success based on merit. He has spent the past 16 years in a wheelchair following a road accident and is believed to be the world's longest surviving quadriplegic. Motor racing is his meat and drink.

Born on 16 April 1942, in South Shields, Frank grew up on Tyneside, but his mother's selfless endeavours enabled him to be educated at St Joseph's College, Dumfries. Young Williams was absolutely determined to find his way into the contemporary motor racing milieu. Trouble was, in those days it was not just a question of finding the key to the door; finding the door itself was a major drama.

In 1964 Frank raced and prepared a crash-repaired F3 Brabham, but eventually concluded that he was not going to make the international front line as a driver, counting himself fortunate to have escaped unscathed when he wrapped the Brabham round a level crossing gate during a race on the wild and woolly Vila Real road circuit in Portugal.

In 1969 Frank and his pal, the brewery heir Piers Courage, decided it was time to go F1 racing.

Williams managed to pull a flanker on Jack Brabham by acquiring an ex-works 1968 Brabham BT24 chassis at the end of 1968. Much to the annoyance of Brabham, whose works cars ran on Goodyear tyres, the Williams Brabham was contracted to race on

Dunlops. Piers really came of age that season, second places in the Monaco and United States Grands Prix testifying to his burgeoning talent. Frank Williams was now poised on the verge of the F1 Big Time. Or so it seemed.

For 1970, the Italian sports car manufacturer Alessandro de Tomaso proposed that his company build a new Grand Prix car which Frank should prepare and enter for Piers Courage to drive.

Progressively the team's efforts improved the de Tomaso, but on 21 June 1970, Piers crashed while running midfield in the Dutch Grand Prix at Zandvoort. The car caught fire and its driver perished in the ensuing inferno. One observer recalls Frank standing in the pit lane after it was all over. Devastated, forlorn, his hopes and dreams torn apart.

Thereafter Frank struggled for many years in the Grand Prix slow lane, eventually selling his team to Austro-Canadian oil millionaire Walter Wolf. But at the end of 1976 he started out from scratch on his own again, founding Williams Grand Prix Engineering. He never looked back.

A decade later, on Saturday, 8 March 1986, Frank's whole world would be upended in a physical turmoil which he would be forced to confront for the rest of his life. On that fateful Saturday afternoon, his rented Ford Sierra plunged off a secondary road into a field between Le Camp and Brignoles, just inland from the coast at Bandol, in southern France and near the Le Castellet racing circuit where he had just been attending the final pre-season tests of the new Williams-Honda FW11 driven by Nigel Mansell and Nelson Piquet.

Williams was travelling with his team manager Peter Windsor at the time. They slid off the road and dropped about six feet into a field. The car overturned and part of the roof collapsed onto Williams, breaking his neck. Windsor was unscathed. Ahead of Frank lay months of treatment and painful therapy, none of which could alter the fact that he was now paralysed from the chest down

Meanwhile, the Williams-Hondas went off into battle, winning a total of nine out of 16 Grands Prix during 1986 as well as the Constructors' World Championship. Yet the boss would not return to the pit lane for almost another year, by which time his company was facing another complex challenge from an altogether unexpected quarter. The Honda management was becoming uneasy about being associated with a company whose boss was almost totally paralysed and this would have fateful long-term implications for their partnership which eventually ended after the 1987 season.

If Williams and Dennis were traditional, dyed-in-the-wool racers, Briatore was as far from that genre as it was impossible to be. The chain-smoking, perennially suntanned Italian spent seven years in the USA setting up Benetton's retail operation, before Luciano Benetton unexpectedly tapped him to head the former Toleman team which Benetton had purchased. "It was very difficult in the US," he remembered. "Nobody knew much about us. I began to think that the only Italian the average American had heard of was Rudolph Valentino. But we had a very aggressive strategy and, after only five years, had something like 750 stores in the US."

What Flavio found in F1 when he took on the Grand Prix job was not totally to his liking.

"Not long after I arrived in F1, I realised something was wrong," he explained. "It was clear to me that Grand Prix racing was no longer sport, but business. We were now talking about teams which employed over 100 people with huge budgets. If you didn't come in from the outside, it was difficult to see the problem. What I quickly realised was that F1 had become media- and television-dependent, but nobody seemed to be trying to do anything to improve the show." Yet many insiders dismissed him as a newcomer who did not really understand what the business was about.

"This is human nature," he shrugged. "When you are in a business, any business, you think you are the best. There is a tendency to think: 'What does this guy from the outside know? He has no experience.' The mentality was that if you are not part of the old generation, you have no knowledge. You are nobody. You don't understand. My response to that was: 'No, perhaps *you* guys don't understand.'"

Briatore would embrace the high life that went hand in hand with his involvement as Benetton's F1 chief, relishing the media attention, particularly the lifestyle magazine features which were attracted to the self-generated air of mystery surrounding him.

He also became a close personal friend of Ecclestone and, indeed, purchased Bernie's former London flat overlooking the Thames at Cheyne Walk.

He eventually left Benetton late in 1997 and his position was taken by David Richards, the founder of the specialist Prodrive rally preparation concern. Their management styles, as things turned out, were as different as chalk from cheese. But Briatore would not be gone for long.

Richards could hardly be more different. He started out aiming to be an RAF pilot and won a provisional university scholarship, only to miss the requisite A-level grades. His father suggested he try accountancy as a business baseline, after which he could perhaps attack something else. It seems to have been sound advice.

"It taught me a discipline which has served me well in business and certainly gave me a direction," he admits. What followed prior to the Benetton job is now a matter of history. Top rally co-driver, then founder of Prodrive, the Banbury-based specialist engineering company which took Subaru to World Rally Championship domination. Amongst other things.

"I want Benetton to have a culture and personality of its own," he said shortly after his arrival on the scene. "I think that, from now on, the personality cult has to be avoided at Benetton. There was a perception from the outside that it was dominated by one individual."

Yet Richards lasted barely a year in the role, unable to resolve differences with the Benetton family over his long-term strategy for the team, which won the 1994 and '95 World Championships with Michael Schumacher.

The Benetton family declined to endorse Richards's new business plan so he immediately tendered his resignation. His position was taken in the short-term by 27-year-old Rocco Benetton, younger son of the Benetton group's co-founder Luciano, who had been working with the team throughout that season. But within months Briatore was back in harness and the decision to sell the team to Renault was announced.

Richards had another agenda he was pursuing with all the resources and energy he could muster. Gravel tracks through dank Welsh forests may not have the obvious appeal of the sun-drenched Monaco harbour front at Grand Prix time, but if Richards has anything to do with it, the rally cars that pound along those slippery byways will become as familiar to television viewers as Michael Schumacher's Ferrari and David Coulthard's McLaren.

Just as Ecclestone transformed F1 from an essentially amateur sport in the early 1970s to the global TV spectacular it is today, so 49-year-old Richards is determined to do the same for rallying. After leaving Benetton, he raised $58.8m by selling 49 per cent of his Banbury-based Prodrive group to venture capital specialists APAX.

It was widely believed at the time that Richards would use at least some of this capital for another foray into F1, possibly involving Prodrive itself, but instead he ended up paying a reputed $38m to purchase the commercial rights to the World Rally Championship from Ecclestone.

When discussing a possible alternative F1 programme with Bernie Ecclestone, the question of taking over the commercial rights to the WRC was raised. Ecclestone said he felt Richards might be interested and a deal was eventually struck for the purchase of International Sportsworld Communications which now promotes and markets the WRC's global TV rights.

"It is my estimation that within five years the World Rally Championship will be perceived as an equal to F1 not only as entertainment, but as a communication platform for manufacturers and sponsors," Richards said. "Yet I predict that both sponsors and car makers will come from a segment of the market sharply differentiated from those who currently compete in F1".

"In TV motorsport terms, the WRC is second only to F1," says Richards, "but, that said, it amounts to only around one-fifth of the F1 exposure. Therefore the growth potential is fantastic.

"That said, I think that if Bernie had been 20 years younger I think he would have taken on the challenge of exploiting rallying's commercial rights and would have done a superb job, even if he had approached it differently."

Prodrive's current main business has been the preparation of the works Subaru rally cars, one of which carried Richard Burns to victory in the 2001 World Rally Championship. Richards removed himself from the day-to-day management of the company he founded in order to concentrate exclusively on promoting rallying as a televised spectacular.

Yet barely two years after acquiring the rally rights, Richards took up another ambitious challenge. He was appointed team principal of the beleaguered BAR-Honda team with a brief to make sense of this unsuccessful, lavishly funded operation which had done little since it was founded in 1999 apart from consume hundreds of millions of dollars to no good effect.

BAT had invested more than 150m pounds in the team, which was founded in 1999 and had yet to demonstrate anything more than average midfield potential.

Richards's Subaru rally cars were backed by 555, another BAT cigarette brand, and the tobacco company had developed a high regard for the millionaire former co-driver who won the 1981 World Rally Championship with Ari Vatanen.

Of course, Briatore and Richards may have been Benetton team principals, but neither was the owner in the same way as Frank Williams or Ron Dennis. Nor was Jean Todt, Ferrari's ascetic team principal who was the driving force behind the team's re-emergence as a winning force in the 1990s.

An introspective and intense individual, Todt was born in 1946, the son of a Polish Jew who escaped to France at the age of 17 and became a doctor. Jean made quite a name for himself as an international rally co-driver, but his big break in management came in 1981 when he was asked by Jean Boillot, head of Automobiles Peugeot, to establish a new competitions department for PSA Peugeot-Citroën.

Todt stayed with the company for more than a decade, overseeing its domination of the World Rally Championship, the desert "rally raids" and the Le Mans sports car classic. Then came the offer from Ferrari which he just could not refuse.

He is a passionate enthusiast for his job – and remains defiantly unapologetic about his controversial race strategies in the 2001 and 2002 Austrian Grands Prix in which Rubens Barrichello was forced to relinquish second and first places respectively to Michael Schumacher.

He also believes that the British F1 teams – not to mention the media – became paranoid about Ferrari's success during the New Millennium. Not that he worries about it unduly.

"In fact, I like that," he said. "It means Ferrari is strong. If Ferrari was not strong, they would feel compassion. Ferrari is a strong, well-organised team, the only one making chassis and engine in-house.

"I respect a lot the English teams, although I don't see the colour of the flag, but I respect strong competitors. I don't understand why they don't respect Ferrari, because I think Ferrari has to be respected. That's my opinion. But if they don't, that's their problem. I don't care. What I care about the most is what is happening inside Ferrari. People stay with the team because it has a good atmosphere inside."

He also fully supports the rationale whereby the reserved and unobtrusive Peter Sauber's team – which uses Ferrari engines – is asked to support the Ferrari standpoint on certain political issues in the sport. And it was the same for Prost in 2001 before the French team went bust. The fact that these two deals added almost $40m to the Ferrari coffers was neither here nor there in Todt's mind.

"Why didn't the others supply them with an engine?" he pondered. "Prost was crying to get a Mercedes engine. He couldn't get them. They would have asked him to follow them (McLaren), to be the B-team and all that. He would have been happy to accept.

"But they did not want to spread their energy or change their present focus. We accepted the commitment, we accepted the danger. In the last race there were six Ferrari-engined cars finishing in the top nine or ten. I think it's a good result.

"They cannot do something against what we think should be the direction. If we are talking about changing to 2-litre V8 engines, for example, they cannot do it against us.

"On some other things, on costs, for example, I would never ask them for something because they pay for engines. It depends on which part of the game we are talking about. For some things they have to follow us, for some others it's up to them."

Further down the Formula 1 food chain sits Eddie Jordan, one of the uniquely extrovert characters within the sport. There is the relaxed, slightly mocking side to the man. Jordan can also be heard shouting mild insults at fellow travellers in the paddock, the guy with the sense of fun and irreverence.

Ron Dennis once described him as "a bit of a rascal" and there are some who believe he lacks the gravitas necessary to be a genuine top F1 operator.

Jordan is very much an Ecclestone disciple. Yet he denies that the fact that Bernie once loaned his company a seven figure sum in order to balance its books means that he is beholden, body and soul, to the commercial rights holder.

"Yes, Bernie has bailed me out once," he says with a stern directness. "But I don't think there is a team in F1 that he hasn't either helped or bailed out. That doesn't buy loyalty, but it helps in the decision-making process. Does that mean that Bernie owns me in the sense of 'can he ring me and get me to sign something without me seeing it?' Not at all."

However, Jordan, along with several of his colleagues, is definitely intimidated by the power of Max Mosley's intellect. In the summer of 2000 the sheer force of the FIA president's personality faced down a challenge to his authority amongst the team principals, which crumbled almost from the moment he glared menacingly at them from the head of the table at the Heathrow Hilton on 30 August.

Of course, Max had been tipped off in advance that several top team bosses – including McLaren's Ron Dennis and Benetton's Flavio Briatore – wanted him to resign his position in charge of international motor racing's governing body.

Mosley also knew very well that the teams had absolutely no chance of getting their way. His position as FIA president owes nothing to the team owners' personal preferences, but to the votes of the 123 countries who make up the membership of the organisation which represents not just motor racing, but motoring interests in general, across the world.

He also knew that handling criticism and dissatisfaction from members of the F1 community went with his badge of office. This most costly and lavish of international sports continued to rely for its success on a complex inter-dependency between the competitors, the governing body and its commercial rights holder Bernie Ecclestone for its success and, by definition, its cash flow.

Predictably, the teams shied away from a direct confrontation, confining themselves to murmurings of vague discontent before knuckling down to the agenda of the day.

"The underlying gripe from the teams seemed to be that they feel the FIA in general, and me in particular, has too much say in the interpreting of rules and running F1 as a whole," said Mosley. "But that's what we at the FIA regard as our job. Writing precise and clear laws has preoccupied people in all walks of life since time immemorial."

In particular, the teams expressed the view that the technical regulations which govern F1 are not clear. Yet again it was hinted that such devices have been used to favour the Ferrari team whom Ecclestone, as F1 commercial rights holder, wanted to see emerge as a serious contender again, in the belief that it would be good for the entire F1 business.

Once more, Mosley fell back on his well-honed mantra. "The Ferrari bias allegations are mildly irritating," he said. "I think there is almost a case for trying to reassure Ferrari that they are not being discriminated against when they see that the president of the FIA, the commercial rights holder, most of the officials and scrutineers are all British."

The notion that the FIA was biased towards Ferrari gained much currency amongst the British constructors. Yet Mosley clearly felt that today's F1 team owners would be well served by developing a more realistic perspective towards the World Championship.

"They go into the F1 paddock where everybody is talking about Formula One, every journalist is writing about F1 and wants to get into their motorhome to talk to them, and they start to think that this is the whole world," he said.

"It isn't. It is a sport – a very important sport – but it's not the whole world. And it's not only not the whole world, it's not actually *their* world. It's actually a world which we've been quietly running for the past 50 years and it's suited them to come into it and it's suited us to have them.

"They entered it because it suits them. As I pointed out to Flavio Briatore, Benetton doesn't have to tell the FIA when they sell their team to Renault. And we don't have to ask Benetton if we sell the (F1 commercial) rights to Bernie or anybody else." Mosley was also dismissive towards suggestions that he and Ecclestone run the sport in the manner of a long-running old pal's act.

"Bernie and I are personal friends, but there are times when I make decisions he doesn't like just as I am sure he makes decisions which I don't like," he said. He also expressed the view that, as things stand, the teams were probably wise enough to realise that they were passengers on a lucrative gravy train.

For their part, the team owners know that Mosley is something of a poacher turned gamekeeper. In 1980, as Ecclestone's legal advisor, he helped frame outline plans for a breakaway F1 series, at a time when the teams were fighting Mosley's predecessor Jean-Marie Balestre for a bigger share of the commercial pie.

In the end, the rival series was a non-starter, teaching Mosley at a relatively early stage that challenging the sport's governing body was absolutely fruitless.

"What we do know from the split between CART and the Indy Racing League in the USA is that the value of two parts is an awful lot less than the value of the whole," he warned.

Mosley recited this piece of theorising almost as a warning shot. Neither he nor the teams believed for a second that anybody was contemplating a rival series. Not for the moment, anyway.

Barely a month after this Heathrow meeting, it looked as though the F1 business might actually be poised on the verge of a minor civil war after Mosley circulated an explosive letter to all the team principals.

The letter, addressed to Frank Williams and Rob Dennis, accused them of going behind the FIA's back and making a direct approach to the European Commission, asking them to insist that motor racing's governing body set up a completely different court of appeal.

This remarkable move by Britain's two top Grand Prix teams technically constituted a breach of the Concorde Agreement. Yet it was a measure of their dissatisfaction with the way the FIA runs the sport that they were prepared to appeal to an outside body in an attempt to change things.

In his letter to Williams, Mosley accused him of trying to disrupt the FIA's negotiations with the EU over the granting to Bernie Ecclestone of a 100-year lease to continue exploiting the F1 commercial rights when the current arrangement expires in 2011.

"It seems difficult to reach any other conclusion," wrote Mosley. "I can quite understand going to the European Commission if all else had failed. What I find more difficult is your doing so when nothing else had been tried. There is a whole process which any reasonable person would go through before seeking to involve an outside agency."

Mosley also accused Dennis of failing to understand how motor racing's infrastructure worked. "He (Dennis) seems to think that he has some sort of mission personally to manage F1," he said waspishly.

"He does not seem to understand that the FIA F1 World Championship belongs to the 120-odd FIA member countries which founded it in 1950 and have run it ever since."

Mosley also suggested that if Dennis wanted to run a motor racing series, then he should start one himself. In reality, the prospect of a pirate series is minute, as Mosley well knew from the FISA/FOCA wars.

The 1981 South African GP staged by the constructors as a pirate race had a scrappy entry and no World Championship status. Technically, it could happen again, but Mosley – better than most – knows it is a remote possibility. So do Williams and Dennis.

Unless, of course, the GPWC series should ever come to fruition. But at the end of 2000, when these explosive incivilities were being exchanged amongst the F1 hierarchy, even the basic announcement of the manufacturers' tentative plans for a new series was more than a year away in the future.

11: SENNA AND SAFETY: A CRUCIAL TURNING POINT

Everybody can remember to the second where they were when they heard of the terrorist outrages of 9/11. Those a generation older can recall how the world seemed to stand still, momentarily frozen in time, when President Kennedy was assassinated. They were both defining moments in contemporary history when one's horror and outrage was mixed with a stark, slightly selfish sense of apprehension. What, one instinctively wondered, comes next?

Such seminal moments of tragedy are thankfully infrequent in motor racing. Pierre Levegh's Mercedes 300SLR scything into the crowd at Le Mans in 1955, killing more than 80 onlookers, is one such disaster. The death of the legendary Jim Clark at a soaking, mist-shrouded, depressing Hockenheim in April 1968 is another. Yet it was the death of Ayrton Senna, following a high-speed accident in the 1994 San Marino Grand Prix, which perhaps shook the sporting world as never before.

Flickering black and white newsreel film still survives of the Le Mans tragedy, but only one person, a trackside marshal, witnessed

Clark's Lotus make its fatal lurch into the pine trees at Hockenheim. The Senna disaster was different; it was played out, second by agonising second, to millions of TV viewers across the world.

Of course, it was not just Senna who perished at Imola. The day before his Williams FW16 speared off the road into the concrete wall at 193mph, F1 freshman Roland Ratzenberger had been killed during qualifying when his Simtek-Ford crashed horrifyingly at an equally ferocious speed. Not since the 1960 Belgian Grand Prix, where British drivers Chris Bristow and Alan Stacey had paid with their lives, had two F1 drivers been killed on a single weekend.

Two weeks later, with the sport still reeling in disbelief as it mourned these two fine men, Karl Wendlinger crashed his Sauber in practice at Monaco. He suffered serious head injuries and for a few more tense and nerve-racking days, it seemed as though he, too, might not survive. Thankfully he eventually pulled through and recovered, but the equilibrium of the Formula 1 business now seemed to be spinning out of control.

Max Mosley was privately shrewd enough to realise that the best thing to do was ride the storm. But on this occasion the Best Thing certainly was not the Right Thing. The sport had to be seen to be taking action. And that's all there was to it.

Hard words were spoken after the tragedy. Senna's great rival Alain Prost expressed the view that the FIA had been deaf to the drivers' concerns on safety issues. Mosley was stung. He immediately rebutted this suggestion.

"I would never refuse to take a phone call from a driver," he said. "I would never refuse to see one. But the only driver who has taken the trouble to come and see me in the last three months and talk about safety is Gerhard Berger.

"After his retirement (at the end of 1993) Alain Prost has said 'we must talk about safety' and I said 'any time.' I've even rung him. But he's never rung back.

"The fact is it (safety) is not fun, and it doesn't make money. So, most of the time, they don't want to do it. In the past, when we've had a drivers' safety commission, when we'd have the first meeting everyone would bother; second meeting, half; and third or fourth they just don't bother.

"It's more fun to go and do a promotion, go skiing or swimming or something. One can understand it. In the end, the drivers' job is to drive. It's our job to see they drive safely. But if it was a question of a driver using a car which was more dangerous, but five seconds a lap faster than the slower one, they would all opt for the quicker one."

In the aftermath of the Senna tragedy, you had to watch for subtle sub-texts coming from the mouths of the leading F1 players. To be frank, many people in F1 felt Mosley's conversion to the motor racing safety cause may have been a Light on the road to Damascus, but that it probably came later in the piece than he himself might have admitted.

Yet safety is an emotive issue; *the* emotive issue attached to motor racing. And just because an individual was not outwardly carrying the safety issue like Jackie Stewart's sacred flame, it did not necessarily mean they were starkly uncaring. Indeed, Mosley would threaten the whole existence of the F1 World Championship by the proposals he set before the teams at Monaco in 1994.

Only two weeks after counselling that the sport should avoid a knee-jerk reaction to Senna's death, Mosley – probably prompted by the Wendlinger accident – did just that. Under the new rules, as from the following race at Barcelona, there would be major restrictions to the aerodynamics – around 15 per cent of total downforce, Max predicted – plus longer-term restrictions on engine power and even more reining in of aerodynamic performance in the longer term.

"Unfortunately, what we wish to put forward does not meet with everybody's approval, so we're going to have to do it despite the Concorde Agreement," he said. "The time has come, because of the gravity of the situation and the force of public opinion, to push aside such considerations and simply do what is right in the general interests of the sport."

Lofty ambitions indeed. The teams sucked through their collective teeth. How would he pull it off? Quite simple. The FIA told the teams that if they did not agree, then the governing body would, quite simply, not run the 1995 F1 World Championship.

Meanwhile, the teams blatantly told Max to his face that he was nuts; that the hastily revised cars would be dangerous. Some weight was given to their claim after the Portuguese driver Pedro Lamy, testing a Lotus 107C at Silverstone, suffered a rear wing failure which the team blamed on the new rules. He was hospitalised with multiple leg injuries.

The mood amongst the teams blackened. Benetton team chief Flavio Briatore gave Mosley a piece of his mind in a letter written on the eve of first practice at Barcelona. "Despite these concerns, you continue to insist on these ill-conceived measures," he told the FIA president. "It is our opinion that the ability of yourself and your advisors to judge technical and safety issues in F1 must be questioned."

When Briatore went on to allege that Mosley's changes actually made the cars more dangerous, Mosley fired a deadly salvo back. If that was the case, he said, the rules meant that Briatore would be responsible for entering a car he knew to be dangerous and there would be consequences. Briatore withdrew the allegation.

Eventually Benetton and eight other teams – Williams, McLaren, Lotus, Pacific, Simtek, Jordan, Arrows and Ligier – all declined to take part in the Friday morning free practice session. Then Mosley warned: "The FIA owns and runs the F1 World Championship. Teams will participate on this basis or not at all."

After a long debate with the teams, he added: "Suggestions that the FIA, or any of its officials, have made concessions or abandoned any powers are wholly false. When you have got serious political journalists writing about recent events in F1, when there are questions in the Italian, Belgian and European parliaments, you must react. With some politicians who are the enemy of motorsport using the occasion to attack us, it became necessary to do something. It was necessary to take the initiative."

Yet the Senna affair would turn out to be one of the most protracted and painful issues for the F1 community. By the autumn of 1996 – more than two years after the accident – the Williams team found itself waiting anxiously to hear whether Frank Williams, technical director Patrick Head and chief designer Adrian Newey would be indicted for alleged manslaughter as a result of Ayrton's death.

In November, reports from an Italian news agency stated that Maurizio Passarini, the public prosecutor in Bologna, had obtained leave from an examining judge, Didier Di Marco, to proceed with an indictment. "Passarini will draw up the indictment in the next few days. Then a date has to be fixed for the trial, which will take place before the local judge in Imola," suggested the report.

Also facing the prospect of legal action were Imola track directors Federico Bendinelli and Giorgio Poggi, FIA race director Roland Bruynseraede and an unnamed Williams mechanic who investigators alleged carried out modifications to the steering column of Senna's car. Under Italian law, a conviction for manslaughter carries a maximum prison sentence of seven years, although a suspended sentence can be applied as an alternative.

The issue of possible legal proceedings against the Williams directors and Imola circuit officials had previously flared up in December 1995, when Professor Enrico Lorenzini of Bologna University, who led the official accident inquiry, hinted that legal action would be amongst the conclusions of the official report.

Yet a year later this official report had yet to be published – and by the end of 1996, neither Patrick Head nor any member of the Williams technical staff had been allowed more than a cursory look at the car in which Senna died. Finally the news was confirmed. In February 1997 the long-awaited trial of Williams and five others on charges of 'culpable homicide' finally began.

The wheels of Italian justice turn painfully slowly. The first day's hearing was purely to consider technical and procedural issues. The hearing was then adjourned for a week. None of the accused were present. Nor did the law require them to be present.

It soon became clear that the prosecution seemed set on pressing home its contention that badly welded alterations to the steering column on Senna's Williams caused a pre-impact failure which sent car and driver into the retaining wall of the flat-out Tamburello left-hander at 193mph.

It seemed that the investigating magistrate Maurizio Passarini lent no credence to photographic evidence, published in the *Sunday Times*, showing Senna about to run over debris on the circuit. It was also suggested that Senna may have pressed too hard on cold tyres after several laps running a much-reduced speed behind the safety car, while debris from a start-line collision between J. J. Lehto's Benetton and Pedro Lamy's Lotus was removed from the straight in front of the pits.

Several drivers had since complained that the race ought to have been stopped immediately, such was the amount of wreckage on the circuit. However, deploying the safety car was a relatively recent device introduced to hold the attention of the spectators – and, more importantly, the television viewers – in precisely such circumstances.

F1 tyres depend on the heat build-up from vigorous use to retain their optimum operating pressures and generate maximum grip. If allowed to cool, they could have lost grip dramatically and created a situation beyond even Senna's control.

Senna had come to Imola vowing that "the World Championship starts here". In the first two races of the season he had experienced nothing but disappointment. He had spun off in front of his home crowd in Brazil as he tried to catch Michael Schumacher's Benetton, then found himself edged off the road at the first corner of the Pacific GP by McLaren driver Mika Hakkinen.

Ayrton was known to be suspicious that there was something

not quite right about his key rival Schumacher's Benetton. Of course, it was subsequently established that this car had an illegal electronic "launch control" system contained within its electronic software systems, but the FIA later accepted that it had not been used.

The implication was that Ayrton might have over-driven in the heat of the moment, his determination to get the better of Schumacher causing him to press too hard before his tyres were up to temperature after several laps behind the safety car. In this configuration, his car might have been particularly nervous to drive over the bumps on the Tamburello corner and this could have contributed to a rare error.

Interestingly, safety-car driver Max Angelelli – himself a racer – told the *Sunday Times* he was very worried that the breathless Opel used for the job was not quick enough. He said a Porsche Carrera RSR would have been more appropriate, and recalls Senna pulling level with him, beckoning him to speed up. "I could see from his eyes that he was very angry," said Angelleli.

There was also speculation that Senna had problems from within his own family. Apparently they wanted him to break up with his current girlfriend, Adriene Galisteu, and Ayrton is believed to have become embroiled in an argument over this matter with his brother Leonardo during the Imola weekend.

The real problem which lay ahead was the prospect of a guilty verdict leaving Italy a "no-go" area for international motorsport. There could be insurance implications, the F1 teams would not wish to attend and the FIA, the sport's governing body, might find it virtually impossible to recruit stewards to officiate at such events.

As Federico Bendenelli remarked after the first day of the trial: "The risk exists that all races in Italian territory will be banned if we are convicted."

Thankfully, all concerned were duly acquitted from the charges in December 1997, but in 1999 another major problem reared its head. The prosecution in the Senna trial decided to appeal against the acquittal of Head and Newey – although not that of Williams – and the date for a new trial was set for November that year.

"I think the Formula 1 teams will probably be very unsettled by this news," said Max Mosley on hearing the news.

"It is a disturbing development not just for Formula One, but for the future of Grand Prix racing in Italy," said Eddie Jordan. "We will be seeking guidance on this from the FIA." Although his acquittal was not the subject of an appeal, Sir Frank Williams asked the Bologna court to include him in the new trial. His Italian lawyer, Oreste Dominioni, said that Williams was seeking exoneration "for the entire team".

The teams were deeply concerned by the fact that there is nothing to stop such a legal action being initiated again by the Italian authorities in the event of another fatal accident in the future. In June 1997, Mosley attended a congress in Rome organised by the European Olympic Committee at which the question of such sporting accidents was debated in detail.

On that occasion he met with members of the Italian judiciary who gave the strong impression that changes to their country's laws in respect of so-called "dangerous sports" would be appropriate. Since then little progress seems to have been made on this issue.

At the time of the original Senna trial, the F1 teams made it very clear that they would have deep misgivings about continuing to race in Italy if the trial judge reached a guilty verdict. The acquittal came as a relief, but news that the appeal was going ahead had rekindled worries that engineers, mechanics and even FIA officials might be very reluctant to attend events in Italy in the future.

This was far from the first time manslaughter charges had compromised the position of Italian motor racing. In 1961 Lotus founder Colin Chapman faced the threat of manslaughter charges after one of his cars, driven by Jim Clark, collided with the Ferrari of Wolfgang von Trips in the Italian Grand Prix at Monza and more than a dozen spectators were killed.

Nine years later Chapman faced similar threats after the Austrian driver Jochen Rindt was killed when he crashed his Lotus 72 in qualifying for the same race. He was eventually exonerated, but not before the works Lotus fielded in the 1972 Italian Grand Prix had to race under a different entrant's name as a legal precaution.

Thankfully, the Senna appeal was a short hearing. On 21 November 1999, the court in Bologna finally rejected prosecution demands for a one-year suspended sentence for manslaughter against Head and Newey.

In rejecting the demand for a sentence, court president Francesco Mirio Agnoli acquitted Head and Newey of the charges, judging that the accusations offered "no proof of blame" on the part of the defendants. Amazingly, this was not the end of the story. In January 2003, just before the text of this volume was nearing completion, the Italian Supreme Court ruled that the *appeal* process of the manslaughter trial must be reopened.

Williams issued a cautiously worded statement on the matter: "Williams today confirms that it has received notice that the Italian Supreme Court has referred the investigation into Ayrton Senna's accident at Imola on May 1, 1994, back to the Court of Appeal in Bologna.

"Williams has assisted in the detailed investigation of this matter over the last nine years and has been cleared of any culpability on two separate occasions. Accordingly, Williams is surprised that the matter should not be considered closed after such an extended period and an extensive examination of all the facts. Williams however respects the legal process in Italy and will continue to fully assist the authorities as they require."

We all remembered how, at the height of the original legal controversy, Max Mosley warned the Italian government that there was a very real prospect that Italy might become a "no-go" area for international motorsport if a manslaughter verdict was reached.

Once again he had to caution the Italian authorities. In reality, of course, further examination of any evidence relating to the accident would be difficult in the extreme as Senna's wrecked Williams, and his damaged racing helmet, were destroyed after the 1999 acquittal as the Court of Appeal ruling seemed to mark the end of the story.

The long-term legacy of the Senna tragedy was twofold. On the one hand it served as a reminder that racing in Italy would always be fraught with legal pitfalls. On the other hand it was a salutary lesson that motor racing can never, ever be totally safe.

It is a cruel illusion to think otherwise.

12: FERRARI SPOILS THE SHOW: BIG CHANGES AHEAD

The scene was the Ferrari motorhome in the paddock at the A1-Ring. It was two hours since Rubens Barrichello had handed victory to Michael Schumacher in the 2002 Austrian Grand Prix yards from the chequered flag and the paddock was in turmoil.

Schumacher had been jeered and booed by the fans. The media was in uproar. Rival team members were aghast at what they regarded as Ferrari's cynical attempt to manipulate the result of the race without any consideration for sporting values.

The season's racing had been processional enough without this drama. Ferrari had the whip-hand over all its rivals, so why did it need to pull a stunt as cynical as this? That was the gist of the prevailing argument.

"It was absolutely disgraceful," said Renault team principal Flavio Briatore. "I've never seen anything like it in 14 years in this business. F1 is much bigger than Ferrari and they should remember it. I shall wait with interest to see whether the FIA does anything about this."

BMW Williams technical chief Patrick Head commented: "It was a cynical manoeuvre." The team's marketing director Jim Wright – a man whose job it is to argue the case for F1's commercial credibility to hard-nosed sponsors – added: "It's farcical, but there is no rule against it. The public reaction from the grandstand says it all."

Ian Phillips, commercial director for the Jordan team, reflected his team's relief that their driver Takuma Sato had emerged unhurt after being T-boned at high speed by Nick Heidfeld's Sauber. But he was scathing in his critique of Ferrari. "It was disgraceful," he said. "I couldn't believe what I was seeing. It makes a farce of the sporting regulations."

Yet Ferrari's sporting director Jean Todt remained defiantly unapologetic as the press and TV cameramen crammed beneath the awning of the team's motorhome, demanding an explanation. A self-absorbed, driven, highly motivated – some would say unsentimental – figure, Todt was not about to be cowed.

Despite howls of indignation, Todt emphasised that Schumacher's title hopes were Maranello's sole overriding priority, which was why he ordered Barrichello to undergo a humiliating repeat of the previous year's race, when he had relinquished second place to Schumacher behind David Coulthard's victorious McLaren-Mercedes.

This time, the two Ferrari F2002s had taken the chequered flag 0.182sec apart, just over seventeen seconds ahead of the Williams-BMW FW24s of Juan Pablo Montoya and Ralf Schumacher, who had been badly let down by the performance of their Michelin tyres at a race where the previous year they both challenged Ferrari for the lead.

It was a bittersweet reward for Barrichello who had earlier in the weekend been celebrating a new contract with the famous Italian team to the end of 2004. Now, after dominating the 71-lap race from pole position, he must have realised that his true role was one of a continuing lackey to the most successful F1 driver of all time.

Todt had wisely decided not to join Michael Schumacher and Rubens Barrichello on the victory rostrum as the crowd in the grandstand opposite the pits roared its disgust.

Schumacher then compounded their diplomatic disaster by making an embarrassed Barrichello take the winner's place on the rostrum while he himself took second billing.

Asked how he felt about the hostile reaction from the spectators, Todt replied: "I am not really bothered. Sometimes difficult decisions have to be taken. We are fighting for a World Championship here and never forget than in 1997, '98 and '99 we lost the Championship at the final race. Some people may not be happy and against us. But at the end of the day it will be more damaging to us if we were to lose the Championship.

"I cannot ask everyone to agree with our decision, but it is our decision. We are only at one third distance in the Championship and two years ago we had three race retirements in a row.

"Rubens was the moral winner, but he offered the victory to Michael for the interests of the Championship. I explained why the decision was taken. Whether it was a right or wrong is another matter. But it may be that by the end of the season people will see it as the right thing to do."

As things would transpire, Todt was deluding himself. Indirectly this heavy-handed strategy would spark the biggest revolution in recent motor racing history. Ferrari's behaviour in Austria was to prove the straw which broke the camel's back.

For an intelligent and extremely adept F1 operator, Todt's lack of judgement seemed crass in the extreme. The purists might have accepted that F1 team management is all about maximising your team's opportunities but, as we will see, the clock was already ticking on F1's credibility. And it was later than Todt clearly thought. Behind the scenes, Bernie Ecclestone and Max Mosley were aware that the sport was in dire need of a makeover. The interest from the paying and viewing public was clearly waning.

Three months later Todt would finally be on the receiving end of a message so blunt that even he could not ignore it. Only 60,000 people – half the usual number – would queue to enter the Autodromo Nazionale di Monza, that hallowed shrine to Italian motor racing, for their home Grand Prix. Even the prospect of a Ferrari 1-2 demonstration run, this time with Barrichello being allowed to win ahead of the blessed Michael, could hardly raise their interest.

Yet for the moment, Todt was having none of this criticism. In a sense, you could see his point. He had painstakingly reassembled the Ferrari squad from the organisational debris he had inherited in 1993, transforming it into a lean, mean fighting machine. Just because McLaren and Williams, his key rivals, were so useless, why should he change his methods of working?

Yet as the sun set on the A1-Ring and the storm clouds gathered to the east, the weather in the Styrian mountains mirrored the sense of unease in the paddock. Many brushed the issue aside as just another F1 storm-in-a-teacup. But others discerned a shimmer of cold apprehension running through the paddock like a hungry dog. Surely it was not possible for Todt to be so insensitive to the wider issues?

For his part, Michael Schumacher sought to pour oil on troubled waters by admitting that he felt distinctly uneasy about being handed victory in such a manner, even though victory in the Austrian race was the only missing achievement on his Formula One CV.

"As Rubens pointed out, this was a team decision," said Schumacher. "Last year, I was sort of involved in the situation because I felt the Championship was much more tight than this year. This year I didn't even think about this and before the race I was asked and I said: 'I don't believe that there is going to be a team strategy involved.'

"And suddenly they told me that he would move over and, yeah, I'm not very pleased about it either. I think none of us is, honestly, but we have to look at the team's ambitions, and the team's ambition is to win the Championship, and you have to secure this because you never know what is going to happen in the next races. Therefore, well, I have to thank Rubens. But obviously I don't take a lot of joy from the victory."

It was ironic that such deplorable behaviour should have come from Ferrari on a weekend when the F1 team principals went through the motions of a meeting designed to improve the F1 business, in particular reining in costs and making the races more interesting.

For its part, the FIA had no immediate comment to make but issued a statement outlining its position and drawing attention to a ruling of the FIA's World Motor Sport Council dating from the summer of 1998.

"It is perfectly legitimate for a team to decide that one of its drivers is its championship contender and the other will support him," read the text. "What is not acceptable, in the World Council's view, is any arrangement which interferes with a race and cannot be justified by the relevant team's interest in the championship."

Whether Ferrari's actions brought the sport into disrepute is another matter entirely and one which the FIA president Max Mosley would have to consider seriously over the following few days.

In fact, F1 only had to wait about 16 hours before Mosley acted. The FIA issued a terse release confirming that Ferrari had been called to explain itself at the following World Motor Sport Council meeting on 26 June.

What really annoyed Mosley was that Schumacher's antics in pushing the hapless Barrichello to the top position on the rostrum, together with the disapproving wolf whistles from the crowd, acutely embarrassed the Austrian chancellor, Dr Wolfgang Schussel, who was on hand to present the trophies.

"I was really struggling to find an analogy in another sport," said Jim Rosenthal, ITV's Grand Prix commentator. "I suppose the closest would be something like Geoff Boycott running out one of his team-mates to gain a century. There were people with tears in their eyes in Austria after Sunday's race, a mixture of disbelief and sadness."

Yet it fell to Damon Hill, the retired 1996 world champion, to put the dilemma facing F1 during the 2002 season into the sharpest and most graphic perspective.

When I telephoned him from Suzuka later in the year, Hill would tell me: "Anyone who has any feeling for the sport feels that we're aching to say something to help put it right. For those of us who love the sport, it hurts. Yet sometimes one feels deeply ashamed to be involved with it. It's embarrassing how far out of touch it's become with all the people involved in it.

"You do have a sense of what a waste, when you watch it. It's lost its way. It's not one thing to put it right, but one thing that would be a good starting point would be for those who run the sport to sit down on a Sunday afternoon and decide whether it's good entertainment."

Then he added thoughtfully: "We don't *have* to have Formula 1 – it's not brain surgery – but it has to do something for them. The most glaring comparison is that with motorcycle racing. The message from everybody in Formula 1 is that they don't give a toss for anyone outside the sport.

"You can fiddle with the regulations until the cows come home, but until there is a fundamental attitude change it shows all the signs of going the way of the Miss World contest."

When it came to it, Michael and Rubens paid a costly price for disrupting the podium ceremony when the Ferrari team and its two most highly paid employees were hit with a $1m fine by the governing body. Half – $500,000 – was payable immediately with the balance suspended for 12 months and payable if there should be a repeat of what the sport's rulers clearly regarded as ill-mannered and inconsiderate behaviour.

A communiqué from the FIA president Max Mosley also reflected his annoyance at the manner in which the team applied its team orders after Barrichello slowed only yards before the finishing line to allow Schumacher the win. "The FIA World Motor Sport Council deplored the manner in which team orders were given and executed at the Austrian Grand Prix," read the statement. "Nevertheless the

Council finds it impossible to sanction the two drivers because they were contractually bound to execute orders given by the team.

"In the circumstances, the Council decided, with some reluctance, that it could take no action over the team orders given." Mosley went on to explain that the Council wanted to impose a penalty which accurately reflected the gravity of the situation.

"We decided it would not be fair to take points away from them," he said. "On the one side, it is true to say it damaged the competition, but on the other side it was legitimate for a team to give such orders because they are competitors.

"The fact that it might destroy a race's spirit has to come second. If a team needs to do everything to win, then they have to do it – except cheating."

Mosley added: "I wanted to impose a sanction for the race itself, but after listening to the discussions and arguments, I was constrained into a position that I could not impose a sanction.

"We could not do anything about the race, so we took the hard line about the podium simply because we do not want to embarrass the country where the Grand Prix is being held.

"The FIA received more emails and faxes on this case than when (Ayrton) Senna died. It completely captivated the public. Ferrari also admitted they were very much surprised by the public's reaction. They are extremely conscious of that and will make sure it does not happen again."

For his part, Bernie Ecclestone admitted that he felt the drivers' behaviour on the podium, when Schumacher pushed Barrichello to the top position, was a little bit stupid.

"I think Michael got into a panic, he'd never been booed before so he reacted," said Ecclestone. "He didn't think it through because he didn't have time to think it through. So I think in the end what has happened is alright. There's an excuse for it but the result wasn't very tasteful."

Although Ferrari's domination of the 2002 World Championship was by this time complete, the situation was dramatically aggravated when Schumacher and Barrichello attempted a side-by-side formation finish in the US Grand Prix at Indianapolis. Ironically for Michael, this misfired and Barrichello snuck across the finish line first by one hundredth of a second.

At Suzuka there was also a team principals' meeting at which harsh words were exchanged. In particular, the Jaguar team principal Niki Lauda told Todt precisely what he thought of him and his efforts to ruin the spectacle of the sport.

"If team orders are going to be imposed in such a stupid way as Ferrari did then, yes, I think it has damaged Formula 1," he said after that meeting. "You could have done the same thing in a more subtle and clever way which wouldn't have hurt everybody so much. The performance of the Ferrari drivers at Indianapolis was particularly silly and that was one of the low points of the year for me.

"What I find pretty boring is this Ferrari one-two strategy which seems to have been adopted over the last couple of years. When you look at the period when Williams and McLaren were dominating Formula 1, the teams used to let their drivers race their asses off against each other – Mansell versus Piquet, Prost versus Senna – and at least we still had fun racing even though it was with the domination of a single team.

"Ferrari have taken all this out of the sport. It is boring and we're now in a situation where nobody watches. We must produce proper racing and it's all Ferrari's fault that we have failed to do so."

Yet as Lauda delivered this rebuke in the pit lane at Suzuka, there was much more to come for the sport to get its head round. FIA president Mosley was on his way to the Japanese race to discuss a mind-boggling memorandum which had been circulated to the teams a few days earlier.

Once the brethren had read the missive, they immediately snapped onto Red Alert. The controversial document amounted to a manifesto from the sport's governing body outlining its plans for a root-and-branch revamp of Grand Prix racing, primarily to address the issues of escalating cost and poor racing in the wake of Ferrari's domination of the previous two seasons.

Of course, Mosley's schoolmasterly side always comes to the fore when dealing with F1 team principals. It is very easy to conclude that he regards them as wayward children unable to see the Big Picture. This slightly patronising – or as one technical director remarked "silver-tongued and gut-wrenchingly paternalistic" – manner of dealing with the team principals manifested itself again in this particular document.

It was couched in kindergarten Janet-and-John question and answer style.

Needless to say, most team principals were stunned. Few took the headline suggestions seriously, yet they immediately detected what Mosley was up to. He wanted to improve the show, so by suggesting a package of seemingly outlandish changes, he knew he would get at least some of them through the crucial F1 Commission meeting which was due to convene on 28 October, two weeks and one day after the final race of the season.

The revised rules were hammered out at a four-hour meeting of the 28-strong FIA Formula One Commission at a meeting at the Heathrow Hilton hotel. However this meeting, which included team principals, race promoters, tyre suppliers and engine manufacturers – in addition to Mosley and Ecclestone – was really the culmination of a succession of meetings held around the world over the last few Grands Prix of the past season.

Yet the FIA backed down from its demands for really radical change which would have changed the basic ethos of F1, most notably the proposal to add "success ballast" to the most successful cars in a bid to slow them down.

"What we had to do was to draw a fine line between not doing enough and doing too much," said Mosley. "On balance, it seems that what we're doing is likely to produce significant change and it would be a mistake to do too much in one go."

From the start of the 2003 season the new rules called for two qualifying sessions, one each on Friday and Saturday, with each car completing a single timed flying lap against the clock on each day. The order in which the competitors take part on Friday is in the world championship points order prevailing prior to the particular race. The running order on Saturday – which establishes the starting grid – sees the fastest driver on Friday taking his run last.

This was designed to produce an unpredictable grid with faster drivers perhaps shuffled further back down the starting order as a result of factors such as oil dropped by cars running earlier in the session or an abrupt change in the weather.

In order to ram home the FIA's intention of outlawing expensive "qualifying cars", it would no longer be permissible to add or remove fuel from the cars' tanks between qualifying and the race. This means that the amount of fuel carried by the cars in qualifying will have to take into account the race strategy anticipated by the team and be sufficient to get through to the first scheduled refuelling stop the following day.

This posed a huge strategic challenge. Does one run on low fuel for qualifying, have a very fast opening stint in Sunday's race and then come in for fuel relatively early? Or does one run with a heavy fuel load in qualifying, risk a lowly grid position and heavy traffic in the early stages of the race in a bid to stay out longer than one's key rivals before refuelling?

Either way, it was certain that every race engineer in the pit lane would be working hard on calculating the best option, right up to the moment where their cars accelerated out onto the circuit for that crucial one-shot qualifying effort.

Williams technical director Patrick Head believed that it could be a really close call with some of the slower cars squeezing up to prominent grid positions if they qualified with a light fuel load. "To take an example, depending on the circuit, last year's Minardi wasn't too bad on speed in qualifying," he said. "So let's say there's 3sec a lap between them, well 3sec is – it depends on the circuit – well 10kg of fuel is somewhere between 0.25sec and 0.4sec.

"At a place like Barcelona it's close to 0.4sec, I think in Australia it's pretty close to that level. Let's say Michael has 80kg in and the Minardi has 10kg, that (difference) represents about 2.8sec, so it could be pretty damn' close."

The new rule brought a quick result. Spain's Fernando Alonso in a Renault became the youngest driver ever to take a pole position, in the second race of the season in Malaysia, the strategy apparently overcoming any inherent superiority of teams like Ferrari, Williams and McLaren.

Championship points are now awarded down to eighth place – previously sixth – on the scale 10-8-6-5-4-3-2-1 in a bid to keep the battle for title placings running further down the field, and longer in the season.

The changes to the testing regulations were more ambitious. Teams were offered the option of restricting their usual testing between Grands Prix to ten days for each of two cars between 1 March and 1 November 2003. In exchange they may test for an extra two hours on the Friday morning of each Grand Prix, when they may use their spare car and a test driver.

The one downside for teams taking up the offer was that rookies starting their F1 career in the 2003 season, such as Brazilian Antonio Pizzonia at Jaguar, now have little opportunity to simply rack up invaluable miles in an F1 car at private testing.

Four teams, at the time of writing, availed themselves of these changes as they regarded the added running at a race venue, at relatively little extra expense to their usual commitments for a race weekend, as a valuable bonus.

One team owner who jumped at the opportunity for an extra two hours in front of a Grand Prix audience was Australian Paul Stoddart, owner of the chronically underfunded but popular Minardi team. Budgetary considerations mean that Minardi does only minimal testing between races in any event, while the bigger teams test for days every other week, sometimes, like Ferrari, with two test teams at separate tracks.

Minardi, joined initially by Jordan, Renault and Jaguar, now has two precious hours to set up its cars to the exact conditions of a Grand Prix weekend, time denied to the other teams. It is notorious in Formula 1 that a car which is brilliant in testing one week may, despite using identical settings, be right off the pace at the same circuit a week later.

Stoddart also spotted another valuable bonus. Permission to use a test driver means he can decide to test a series of promising drivers in real race weekend conditions – at their considerable expense – or put a home-town driver in the spare car for valuable exposure and sponsorship.

"This is the first time that a test driver will be able to pit himself against the team's regular driver in identical cars at the same time on the same circuit," Stoddart added.

David Richards, team principal of British American Racing, hailed the changes as being "all a triumph of commonsense". He added: "Most important of all, everybody in the meeting was in unison about these changes. We were all behind the revamp of the qualifying format but there was a little more discussion on the matter of testing limitations.

"As far as changes to the cars are concerned, I would say we must bite off one chunk at a time. We will be considering all that in just over a month's time."

Niki Lauda, the Jaguar team principal who was soon to be fired from that role in one of the British team's periodic management reshuffles, said he was happy with the changes. "Now we have to address other elements including changes to the circuits," he said. "We will also consider changes to the technical regulations to improve overtaking.

"I personally favour slashing aerodynamic downforce and going back to slick tyres, but perhaps that's because I raced on those and I know about them at first hand."

Yet this was as nothing compared with the announcements made by the FIA on 15 January 2003. Frustrated that, in his view, the teams had made no meaningful effort to grasp the question of restricting long-term costs in F1, Mosley moved unilaterally to break what he saw as an increasingly frustrating deadlock.

In yet another day-long meeting at a Heathrow Airport hotel, the ten team principals met with Mosley and Ecclestone to discuss a package of rules designed to change the face of Grand Prix racing. After a season highlighted by processional racing and dwindling television audiences against a backdrop of a dominant Ferrari team whose drivers were instructed not to compete against each other, Ecclestone and Mosley effectively forced the teams to go back to basics.

Traction control, the anti-wheelspin device which offered maximum grip to the driver and has resulted in the cars cornering seemingly on rails for the past two seasons, would be phased out as soon as possible, perhaps during the course of the 2003 season and certainly before the start of 2004. There would no longer be any radio communication between the pit wall and the drivers and only two cars per team would be permitted from the start of the season. That meant no spare cars would be deployed by any teams as back-ups in the event of one of the machines being involved in an accident.

"There is nothing wrong with the technical development in Formula One, it is just a case that some teams cannot afford to compete at the current level," said Ecclestone. "The problem is that the team principals have lost control. It is the engineers, and in some case the drivers, who run the teams. If the team principals stop them playing with their hobby, which is each of them trying to prove to their counterparts in other teams that they are the best, the top people will leave for another team which will support their desire to be the best.

"We must change the regulations in a way that stops engineers being able to spend unnecessary money, which does not in any way relate to improving the Drivers' World Championship, the sport, or our duty to entertain. We have 300 million people who watch our sport on TV and who really don't care about electronics or how many cylinders the engines have. Teams have reached a peak of income for the moment. They must now, as most companies have done, reduce costs."

Mosley admitted that the governing body cannot change any rule for 2003 without the unanimous agreement of the teams. It seems that the teams all agreed – some albeit with reservations – after Mosley made it clear that the application of Article 61 of the sporting rules – namely that a driver must drive the car without any assistance – would be rigorously applied.

Although the FIA was prepared to allow the teams some grace in getting rid of traction control and launch control systems, it intended to apply Article 61 in a "zero tolerance" manner, he said. "Severe constraints will be placed upon electronic control of throttles, clutches, differentials and actuators," Mosley continued.

"Each team must be able to demonstrate compliance (to these rules) without (computer) software inspection. That's to say it must be obvious that there is no such system on their car. But if it can be shown that immediate full compliance to these rules will cause more costs because the start of the current season is so close, then the FIA is prepared to allow a derogation for all or part of 2003. But it will be enforced for 2004."

If necessary the FIA was prepared to impose the use of a standard, approved ECU (electronic control unit) for all engines which would enable the governing body to be sure that the rules were being respected. On a longer-term basis there would be a requirement for standardised braking systems for 2004, a standard specification rear wing for all cars and an obligation that all engine manufacturers involved in F1 also support a second team, as proposed by Mercedes-

Benz ahead of this meeting.

So what difference would these F1 rule changes *really* make? Would we see a whole new generation of rising stars blossoming at the wheels of a new breed of Grand Prix car, with opposite-lock slides and tyre smoke the order of the day? Would we see Michael Schumacher dislodged from his position of domination astride the global winners' rostrum? Or would the race fans be treated to wheel-to-wheel finishes at most of the races?

The reality, of course, was a little more measured. Simply depriving the cars of a selection of electronic gizmos and forcing Schumacher and his pals to flick the finger-tip gearchange paddles on a semi-automatic – rather than totally automatic – gearbox, was not going to make a whole lot of difference.

The driving brilliance and natural feel which are essential elements of a great driver's repertoire would in no way be changed by these rule changes. Just as with Fangio's domination at the wheel of a Mercedes W196 or a Maserati 250F four decades ago, so Schumacher will continue to be the best, no matter what car he is driving.

What the new rules would mean is that – in the pouring rain, for example – the German ace now had even more scope to demonstrate that genius in a more spectacular manner, correcting a succession of slips and slides with minuscule adjustments to his steering wheel. Excellence would still be rewarded.

Almost. Schumacher seemed somewhat rattled in the opening races of 2003, admitting that he preferred being able to use every possible electronic gimmick to perfect his car. And, despite still having traction control, the acknowledged "rainmaster" slid off the road like a rookie in the sodden Brazilian Grand Prix. But it was not long before he was back to his winning ways.

Fundamentally, what these rule changes delivered was a slightly more even playing field. Nobody in their right mind suggested that Jordan or Jaguar would suddenly, magically, be capable of going head-to-head with Ferrari, Williams or McLaren. Yet by curbing some of the top teams' lavish spending, the new rules will at least rein in some of the advantages which accrue simply to those who are able to spend their way to competitiveness.

Again Mosley's tactics of announcing a raft of rules with the objective of getting a few key issues through became evident. On 2 May, after intensive talks with team principals and their technical directors, the new rules were changed again.

While automatic gearboxes and launch control were still banned for 2004, electronic traction control was reprieved. The teams argued successfully that if it were banned, the engine companies would simply spend fortunes on a mechanical system.

But Mosley got the quid pro quo he really wanted, for the future of the sport. "The FIA agreed," a statement said, "on the clear understanding that this would enable the engine manufacturers to supply the independent (smaller) teams with engines at a fully affordable cost, having regard to the current economic climate."

It would be a major factor in the survival of the smaller teams, necessary if for no other reason than to make up the numbers and variety of the field, and might even encourage new teams to come into F1 again. In the heyday of the (relatively) economical and long-lived Ford-Cosworth DFV, F1 fields had risen to 36 cars, so many that the FIA had to introduce a "pre-qualifying" shoot-out to decide which of the new teams should be allowed into the 26-car qualifying sessions.

If affordable engines "were indeed available to all teams from 2004 onwards", the FIA continued, it would drop its proposals, bitterly opposed by the engine manufacturers, that the same engines would have to be used for up to six races in 2005/2006. One manufacturer had growled that multi-race units would be "tractor engines", not the brilliant technology they wanted to showcase.

The teams also won a reprieve for car-to-pit telemetry, also on cost grounds – it can warn of an engine about to fail before it does so, saving the cost of a destroyed engine – and other concessions.

However, after all these lofty promises, at the end of the day Mosley did a U-turn against his better judgement and the FIA decided to permit traction control systems on an open-ended basis. It was decided that the scope for cheating against a ban was just too great and the problems this would cause with endless arguments and protests was not worth the trouble. He did, however, make this contingent on the manufacturers agreeing to guarantee sufficient engine supply deals to make sure no team needed to go out of business from 2003 onwards.

At the Heathrow meeting there had also been a degree of behind-the-scenes largesse deployed by Ecclestone and the rival teams, who agreed to re-direct a few million dollars in the direction of Jordan and Minardi to ensure that they remained in business. This all made good business sense for the front runners, because if the field falls below 20 cars then they are obliged to make up the numbers by offering to field third cars, a much more expensive option than offering a helping hand to their less fortunate colleagues.

"In my 12 years of Grand Prix racing, I don't think there has ever been such a significant meeting," said Eddie Jordan. "I think everybody in the meeting was committed all round to helping each other. The atmosphere was the best I have ever known. Max had to be quite brutal in enforcing cost-cutting moves over the next three seasons, but generally I have never seen such a positive meeting. The cars will be more exciting to watch without the driver aids."

Paul Stoddart added: "What it proved is that Bernie, the FIA and all the other teams are committed to ensuring that independents like Eddie (Jordan) and myself stay in business.

"The rule changes make sense and will contribute to good cost savings over a long period. This meeting has proved that the governing body is taking the issue of costs seriously and has taken steps to secure the sport's future."

Yet, when it came to it, that magical financial lifeline would never materialise.

The plans were greeted with a wide range of emotions from the team principals when they were confirmed. Ferrari's Jean Todt was certainly not pleased by the news.

"I wouldn't say we've got Ferrari's unqualified support by any means because some of these things could be seen as being quite detrimental to them," said Mosley. "On the one hand even Ferrari is coming under pressure to reduce costs, but on the other hand they are now saying 'we've got all these systems in place and we can't use them.' But whatever you decide as a cut-off point this sort of problem will always be the case.

"McLaren was absolutely against it and I think Ron Dennis went into shock when he realised what we were proposing."

Many Formula 1 insiders remained deeply sceptical of the FIA's claims to a firm line, believing that the governing body has shown partiality towards the Ferrari team on too many occasions in the past, compounding the atmosphere of suspicion and distrust.

Mosley branded this as arrant nonsense. "When Ferrari was losing – and bearing in mind that they are the best-known brand in Formula One – you could imagine people saying that, for commercial reasons, at least Bernie Ecclestone, and possibly the FIA, would want to help them win.

"But when it gets to the stage that their top driver is on the podium at every race for more than a season, they are sweeping the board and winning everything, and where people are switching off the television because of Ferrari, then anybody who believes that we are helping them must be mad, because we would be sawing off the branch we're sitting on.

"In fact, we've never been partial to Ferrari and the main basis for that accusation is the famous bargeboard test where McLaren screwed up their case."

Mosley was referring to the 1999 Malaysian Grand Prix where the Ferraris of Eddie Irvine and Michael Schumacher were disqualified from first and second places due to a dimensional infringement on the aerodynamic deflectors on the side of their chassis. This gave victory to Mika Hakkinen's McLaren-Mercedes, but Ferrari appealed the decision and were reinstated after the FIA Court of Appeal hearing.

"If McLaren had taken the point they should have taken, they would have won the case," said Mosley. "Had they asked Ferrari to prove that their deflector was at the correct angle on the car, they couldn't possibly have done it because it had been removed from the car. But McLaren didn't take that point.

"I can't go in to argue McLaren's case; if they screw up, they screw up. Anyway, it's manifest nonsense (that we have shown partiality) after what has happened over the last two seasons."

McLaren was furious at this off-hand dismissal of what they regarded as a gross miscarriage of justice and material misinterpretation of the evidence by the FIA Court of Appeal. But they kept their counsel. They also felt that Mosley had missed the fundamental point. They had only been invited along as witnesses to that Court of Appeal. The main issue was between Ferrari, the appellant, and the governing body. If they were convinced that Ferrari had been shown bias, they were also privately of the view that the FIA's lack of partiality extended to regarding the McLaren organisation as an easy target.

They felt that the governing body was just waiting for them to stray slightly out of line before slapping them down. It was certainly an uneasy relationship and Mosley did little to allay their apprehension.

Yet for all its caution, McLaren thought the imposition of these rules as definitely a move too far. After consulting with their colleagues at Williams, the two British blue riband F1 teams decided to challenge the FIA by taking the question of these new rules to arbitration barely a fortnight before the start of the 2003 season. Their action was greeted with dismay by some rival team principals who believed that the last thing Formula One needed was a major legal dispute only two weeks before the first race of the season in Australia.

"I am horrified and absolutely astounded," said David Richards of British American Racing. "This is the last thing the sport needs at the moment. We should all be pulling together to make it a success."

Paul Stoddart, struggling to finalise even a 38 million dollar budget, modest by contemporary F1 standards, was also deeply concerned. He commented: "I've got so much to say but I'm not going to say anything. It is a very sad prospect if we are going to have a year of off-track politics when the fans would rather have on-track racing."

McLaren and Williams reiterated their accusation that Max Mosley was trying to "dumb down" Formula One with the new measures.

They accused Mosley of breaching the sport's own rules, which he himself was largely responsible for framing, and took their complaint to the International Chamber of Commerce in Lausanne, the agreed court of last resort under the terms of the Concorde Agreement.

"We could conceivably have proceeded against the FIA in the French civil courts," said Martin Whitmarsh, the McLaren managing director, "but we are not seeking to be confrontational in this matter. We just want it clearly established that the Formula 1 rules have to be applied in the manner which has been agreed."

The International Chamber of Commerce would consider the matter in front of three impartial adjudicators, the appointment of whom has to be approved by all the litigants. Under the agreed terms of the Concorde Agreement, their verdict is legally binding on all the parties although the FIA was quick to point out that such rulings were not retrospective.

The dispute resolution mechanisms developed by ICC have been conceived specifically for business disputes in an international context which may entail problems of different legal and cultural systems. For all these reasons, national courts in the country of one of the parties may not appear suitable to the other parties. The ICC, as an international body, provides a neutral ground for appraising disputes.

"They are quite entitled to take the action they have," said Mosley, "although we regard the matter as something of a storm in a teacup." He added that the FIA had taken legal advice on the issue and was confident of its position.

Specifically the two teams criticised the FIA rule changes on the grounds of safety, saying that the new regulations whereby cars must be kept in a secure *parc fermé* between Saturday night and the Sunday race morning, where no work can be carried out on them, would cut time for technical preparation and therefore have a potentially adverse impact on safety.

Yet Dennis's candour would catch him out yet again. In a business where speaking one's mind oh-so-often needs to be tempered by subliminal second thoughts, the McLaren boss consistently refuses to toe any party line out of pure expediency. His latest pronouncement was that, if there was to be a fighting fund to save struggling teams, then Jordan was a more deserving case than Minardi.

"I feel strongly that what help is given to those two teams should not be equal as I don't see them as equals in Grand Prix racing," he said. "Jordan have a long-established history of competing in Grand Prix racing, led by a colourful and aggressive individual whose skills of survival are finely honed. While he has been known to have a degree of vocal complaint, this pales in comparison to that of Paul Stoddart, who has little track record in F1."

Paul Stoddart was, not surprisingly, less than impressed with Dennis's remarks. Yet many rival teams privately shared Dennis's concerns that the Australian airline boss simply could not make a success of the F1 business.

"The thing about Paul is that he's always round with the begging bowl," said one team owner. "And if you give him a hand-out, you always suspect that he'll be back in a couple of months for another couple of million dollars."

13: WHO GETS THE BRITISH GRAND PRIX?

I t was on the evening of 5 December 2001, that the telephone rang in the London offices of FIA president Max Mosley in a quiet street just off the Fulham Road. Mosley's secretary took the call and put Sir Jackie Stewart through to her boss for a highly charged conversation over the future of the British Grand Prix.

Stewart, the president of the British Racing Drivers' Club which owns Silverstone, was speaking from the office at his country home in rural Buckinghamshire.

He was expressing acute anxiety to Mosley over rumours he had heard during the course of the day to the effect that the FIA's world motorsport council, which was due to meet the following Friday in Monte Carlo, was toying with the notion of downgrading the British race to non-championship status.

"Why would you seek to to do that, Max, at a time when Silverstone is more committed than ever to upgrading and improving the circuit for Formula 1?" asked Stewart.

Stewart was referring to the planned $60m programme of improvements intended to come on stream in 2003, jointly funded by the BRDC, the race promoters Octagon Motorsports and Bernie Ecclestone in his role as Formula 1's commercial rights holder.

The deal was that Octagon would write the original cheque and the BRDC would chip in its percentage by taking a reduction on its $12m annual circuit rental from the race promoter. Ecclestone's notional contribution would be a reduction in the race's sanctioning fee – a confidential figure – for a period of five years.

Mosley's response to Stewart's impassioned plea was not recorded in specific detail, but FIA insiders strongly suggest that the FIA president indicated to Stewart that the governing body was approaching the end of its patience with Silverstone.

"It's always jam tomorrow with Silverstone," said one source close to Mosley, "but the only jam they seem capable of producing is a traffic jam."

It was the latest exchange in a long-running battle over the future of a race whose critics believed was being held at a venue long past its sell-by date and its supporters who remained confident that its greatest days as a world-class motorsports venue were still to come.

The conversation between Mosley and Stewart came after three months of intensive lobbying behind the scenes as both the FIA president and the former triple world champion privately assessed the best way to resolve an increasingly complex dilemma.

Silverstone had been roundly castigated by the governing body for the flooded car parks in 2000, but despite assurances that things would be better the following year, the FIA was still not happy about the traffic flow.

The governing body demanded more be done for 2002 and, at that highly charged meeting at Monaco, made clear to the Silverstone promoters that if access to the track was not further improved, then the race's long-term future would be permanently jeopardised.

Mosley's mood was not improved on the morning of 6 December when he opened a copy of the Italian newspaper *Il Corriere dello Sport* to see more criticism of Silverstone under the heading "One of the most prestigious Grands Prix pays the price for its disastrous organisation over the last few years".

A member of the newspaper's staff suggested: "There are many other countries that clearly suggest that Max and Bernie favour the British Grand Prix and let the organisers get away with things that nobody else can.

"Paradoxically, that puts pressure on them to force Silverstone to deliver – or alternatively give them the chop."

That may have been true, of course, but then Mosley was always an adept politician. Nevertheless, the downside risk for any politician is that their earlier remarks are all too frequently quoted back to them.

Certainly Mosley's attitude over Silverstone was a case in point. After all, barely two years had passed since the FIA president offered generous praise about the British GP venue when he wrote in celebration of the circuit's 50th anniversary:

"Silverstone has had a fantastic 50 years and for many people it sums up the greatness and long traditions of British motorsport. Many legends and champions have been born on this circuit and I hope this proud tradition continues for years to come.

"The circuit, in recent years, has been going from strength to strength, building on its proud heritage and boasting facilities and services that are at the top of their class.

"One can attribute this success to the people who have been managing and investing in the circuit and their ability to move with the times."

It seemed stretching objective credibility to believe that things had so dramatically changed for the worse in a little over two years. But then that was only part of the story.

Meanwhile, as Stewart and Mosley chatted, 25 miles down the

road at Brands Hatch, Rob Bain, the chairman of Octagon Motorsports, was sitting in his comfortable office suite overlooking the fast Clearways right-hander on the race circuit which last hosted the British Grand Prix in 1986.

The irony of his situation could hardly have escaped him. After the sodden debacle of the 2000 British Grand Prix, held on an unseasonably early Easter weekend, Brands Hatch had originally been due to host the race in 2001.

"It won't happen here," Bain had triumphantly predicted with reference to Silverstone's mud-caked car parks and access roads as he looked forward with confidence to moving the race to Brands Hatch. Unfortunately, Bain was right, but not for the reasons he expected.

It was the race – not just the car parking chaos – which didn't happen at Brands Hatch because the track couldn't get the necessary planning permission. So Octagon found itself entering into a 15-year deal to stage the British Grand Prix at Silverstone which was on course to cost Bain's employers around $190m over the period of the contract.

Suddenly, in the late afternoon of 5 December, the Octagon Motorsports switchboard was jammed with calls from the media demanding comments on the rumours that his race was about to be ditched by the FIA. Bain handled the media inquiries with all the delicacy of a bomb disposal specialist. Officially, he reacted with absolute neutrality, pointing out that the rumours came from no firmly attributed source.

Yet he was worldly enough to guess that they had almost certainly been leaked from the FIA, perhaps with Mosley's approval, as a direct means of communicating a subliminal message; Silverstone is drinking at the last-chance saloon, so do something about it.

Bain, along with the BRDC who had leased Silverstone to Octagon Motorsports as part of the deal to guarantee the race's future, knew that they had to keep a low profile and not ruffle any feathers.

Clearly some degree of government funding or assistance would seem to be a convenient way out of this dilemma, although given Tony Blair's embarrassment over the 1m-pound donation from Ecclestone in 1997 the government could have been forgiven for being sceptical about helping a sport which seems awash with cash and wall-to-wall private jets

Mosley shrewdly took the point. "I wouldn't feel at all comfortable asking for public money for work on the circuit itself, or its infrastructure," he said.

"What we feel the government *could* do is to make sure the Silverstone bypass is completed in time for next year's British Grand Prix, give the necessary consents to enable Octagon to build the spur road leading to the track entrance and to have traffic plans in place that take full advantage and benefit of the new road layout."

Privately, Octagon kept its nerve and remained confident that the FIA would look favourably on a confidential report which would be delivered to the World Motor Sport Council detailing the progress on traffic flow made in time for the 2001 race. By any standards, this was a nerve-racking period.

It was hard to believe that just over two years had passed since Brands Hatch Leisure plc announced that it had formalised an offer to Bernie Ecclestone's Formula One Administration organisation to host the British Grand Prix at Brands Hatch from 2002 – in the event that Silverstone would not sell out to its rival organisation.

That deal was announced on 30 March 1999 with just over two years to run before the existing contract with Silverstone was set to expire.

Brands Hatch Leisure also pointed out that it had already entered into an *exclusive* contract with Formula One Administration which secured the British Grand Prix at Silverstone until 2009 in the event that BHL acquires Silverstone from the British Racing Drivers' Club.

Meanwhile, an internal battle to restructure the BRDC saw two high-profile celebrities, Jackie Stewart and the 1979 world champion Jody Scheckter, coming out firmly in opposition to the proposals.

Scheckter, the last man to win the World Championship in a Ferrari 20 years ago, circulated to all the club's members an open letter objecting to the proposed changes.

He contended that the new proposals would make Silverstone more vulnerable to potential takeovers in the future, not less so. In particular he took issue with the plan which would see a new company – Silverstone Circuits Group – established to own the commercial businesses of the BRDC which are currently operated by two separate companies, Silverstone Circuits and Silverstone Estates.

"If the proposed scheme goes ahead the club says that it will have a golden share which it can use as a veto for the first three years," said Scheckter. "Even with a 10 per cent maximum shareholding permitted, it means four or five members could get together to control the club's destiny.

"I do not understand the logic of this plan. I believe it is making the assets more vulnerable. The only thing I think this restructuring achieves is to put some money into the pockets of the members, to take control of the BRDC assets outside of the club and the end of the BRDC as we know it."

His letter was countersigned by an impressive group of international racing personalities including Stewart, Le Mans sports car veteran Derek Bell, team owner Sir Frank Williams and his technical director Patrick Head, McLaren technical director Adrian Newey and Colin Vandervell, millionaire son of the late Tony Vandervell whose Vanwall Grand Prix cars won the first Constructors' World Championship in 1958.

Stewart added: "As a vice president of the club I have told (Lord) Alexander Hesketh (the president) that I unfortunately cannot agree with the proposed plan. I share Jody's concerns that there is just no guarantee beyond three years over the club's control."

The dissenters also pointed out that issuing shares would play into the hands of Brands Hatch Leisure. With a shareholder base Foulston would have something more tangible to target at a time when she was making no bones about the fact that she would canvass every BRDC member individually, wherever they were in the world, to ensure that her bid was successful when it was eventually launched.

The current contract for the British Grand Prix at Silverstone expired in 2001 and the BRDC had not obtained a renewal as part of the restructure proposals which were finally implemented.

Brands Hatch Leisure claimed that in the event that the restructure proposed was adopted by the BRDC members this would have the effect of triggering the "change of control" clause within the existing Grand Prix contract.

Nevertheless, Foulston commented critically about the BRDC's commercial acumen. "The non-commercial approach to date has put in jeopardy the very existence of the Grand Prix in Britain," she said. "We have the financial ability and commercial expertise not only to support the British Grand Prix but also to undertake the necessary investment into the host circuits' infrastructure."

Foulston had already proved herself to be quite a shrewd player on the British Grand Prix scene. The chief executive of Brands Hatch Leisure was certainly no shrinking violet. She was a feisty and gregarious 31-year-old millionairess with an open manner and a ready laugh.

Brands Hatch was originally purchased by John Foulston, Nicola's father, in 1986. He was the millionaire head of the Atlantic Computers company and a keen amateur racer in his own right. Tragically, he was killed testing an historic Indianapolis McLaren at Silverstone the following year.

"He had put the circuit into a family trust," recalled Foulston. "At the time I was 22, I knew everything and asked the trustees to be given the chance to run the company. John Webb, who'd run Brands Hatch for Motor Circuit Developments – the previous owners – said 'I

don't want to stay if Nicky's here' and that's how I got the opportunity to be chief executive.

"However, when that happened, there was obviously a concern
that I was very young and didn't know enough about business, so
they put the land itself in a trust separate from Brands Hatch Leisure.
But I found it difficult to work with the trustees, so I bought the
business of Brands Hatch Leisure from the trustees in 1992 when I
was 24.

"Then in 1995 I bought out the freehold, which is where the
venture capitalists APAX came on the scene, after which we launched
the group on the stock market."

Yet Foulston's stated ambition sent shudders of indignation
through the massed ranks of the British Racing Drivers' Club, the
owners of Silverstone. They were equally determined to spare no
efforts to see the impertinent Ms Foulston thwarted in her personal
ambitions.

However, Foulston may have an ace card up her sleeve in the
form of tacit blessing from F1's commercial rights holder Bernie
Ecclestone. Motor racing's most powerful entrepreneur has been seen
as effectively endorsing BHL's bid for Silverstone, hinting that Britain
could lose its round of the world championship if the circuit didn't
smarten up its commercial act. Foulston believes that should be a
matter of deep concern for everybody involved in professional motor
racing.

"That is a whole different ball game," she said seriously. "If the
Grand Prix leaves the UK that will have an adverse effect on the
whole of British motorsport. In that situation we would step in and
secure the event. We would rebuild Brands Hatch, although how
much needs doing is a matter of some debate.

"It obviously needs a lot of work, not least because we want to
be able to look after 200,000 customers. But safety developments
have moved on enormously since we last held a Grand Prix here and
there are many different ways of enhancing this issue. Everybody

says that this is impossible, but nothing is impossible.

"We wouldn't be changing the face of Brands Hatch as we know it."

She also made the point that none of her rivals could seek any consolation in the notion that she might have problems with planning permission if she sought to upgrade Brands Hatch.

"There is no problem there," she said. "We have planning permission as a motor racing circuit and all we would be doing is precisely that. There is no change of use involved." Yet Foulston would eventually be proved incorrect in this contention.

In any case, re-developing Brands Hatch was very much Foulston's back-stop plan. Her first priority was for BHL to take over Silverstone, to which end Ecclestone had granted her the right to run the British Grand Prix at its current venue should she be successful in her takeover quest.

"What we are talking about is the development of British motorsport over the next 50 years," she said firmly, "and what we can do about taking on football and the other major sports in terms of attendance and coverage.

"I will therefore work very hard to give my vision an airing to all BRDC members, and I believe that once they hear the proposals in detail they will see that it is a balance, a partnership, we are proposing. It's not just a question of buying a circuit."

Foulston characterised the issue in starkly simple terms. "There are two jobs to do," she insists. "On the commercial management of Silverstone circuit, we can definitely do a better job than the current management team at Silverstone.

"The other job that needs doing is the protection, development and organisation of motorsport. The BRDC can do a better job at that than we are currently doing on our own circuits. I believe that is what their focus should be for the future."

Foulston's approach was absolute anathema to the BRDC old guard, although the club membership was privately divided over the best way forward to preserve its long-term interests.

Initially the BRDC vigorously challenged Foulston's plans which were buttressed by a lavish PR onslaught over the weekend of the 1999 Monaco Grand Prix when she offered to fly several national journalists, including the author, *back* from Monaco on the Friday just to hear her formal business briefing on the subject. It was an invitation that I declined.

It looked as though she was in a strong position. Ecclestone added his two pennyworth, casually commenting that he had "offered the BRDC the opportunity to renew their contract but they felt they were not in a position to do so.

"The British Grand Prix has been saved. If we had not done the deal with Nicola, these people (the BRDC) would not have agreed and the British Grand Prix would have gone.

"Basically (Silverstone) is like a big club race. They've built some new grandstands, but it's all a bit run-down, a bit Battle of Britain-ish."

However, while it was known that Silverstone baulked at the prospect of paying an increased annual fee of $11.5m – plus 10 per cent annual increases over the five-year period – to renew their contract, BRDC spokesman Peter Gaze denied they had turned down a formal offer.

"Silverstone is still in pole position to host the British Grand Prix from 2002," he said. "Brands Hatch do not have the facilities to stage a Grand Prix. Silverstone is the only venue to accommodate it."

Lord Hesketh added: "we are not going to commit the club to financial suicide. Today, if we didn't have the British Grand Prix we could continue to run this club in exactly the same way. The truth is we have got to have a negotiation which is sensible (over the race). Who can predict what the state of Formula 1 will be in ten years' time?"

Foulston, meanwhile, had speculatively committed around 20 million pounds to upgrading Brands Hatch which last hosted the British Grand Prix in 1986. However, Formula 1 insiders continued to

remain sceptical as to the financial viability of her planned programme, feeling that Brands Hatch Leisure could over-stretch its
resources depite increased credit facilities of $48m from its bankers,
the Bank of Scotland.

They also pointed out that less than a month had passed since
Foulston indicated that running the British Grand Prix at Brands
Hatch was a fall-back position in the event of her failing to purchase
Silverstone from the BRDC.

Some believed that her announcement of a deal to run the race
at Brands Hatch after all was merely a means of forcing the BRDC
board back to the negotiating table to continue discussions to sell
her their track.

Irrespective of the outcome of this elaborate game of posturing,
the one certain winner seems to be Ecclestone's empire which had
received a letter of credit from Brands Hatch guaranteeing payment
of the first year's fee for the British Grand Prix under the terms of
Foulston's new deal.

Meanwhile, McLaren team managing director Ron Dennis
entered the high-profile debate by slamming Foulston's plans during
the Monaco Grand Prix weekend.

He branded her strategy in announcing that she had signed to
run the race at the famous Kent circuit as deliberately designed to
"destabilise" the British Racing Drivers' Club.

"There is a very emotional and hotly debated issue over this in
Britain, but some people have to stand up and be counted," he said.
"What is happening is wrong.

"People need to understand that the BRDC has got some relatively mature people at the top who are perhaps a little too mature
and need to stop fighting by Queensberry Rules and take a more
aggressive stance in defending their club."

Dennis's main objection centres round the fact that the
Silverstone organisers are "almost unique" in reinvesting their revenues in the sport.

Just over six months later, in January 2000, Foulston resigned as CEO of Brands Hatch Leisure. By then the company had been sold Octagon, a subsidiary of the US Interpublic Group, for $192m.

Foulston had checked out with a personal fortune of around $40m. End of story. Ecclestone sounded a little bewildered by this move.

"I must say I was a little surprised at the news of her departure," said Ecclestone who had personally signed the deal with Foulston to give Brands Hatch the rights to the British Grand Prix.

"I don't think it will make much difference to the situation. They have a contract, and when they get their planning consent, and do the necessary work to the circuit, then they will get their race."

"It is business as usual," said a Brands Hatch spokesperson yesterday confirming that the Octagon Group, the US sports and promotional group which purchased BHL Leisure the previous year, would press ahead with plans to update the circuit.

Meanwhile, Silverstone's owners contemplated running the 2000 British Grand Prix on an unseasonably early Easter Sunday, following a winter which had seen some of the heaviest rainfall in history.

Easter bank holiday weather may well be the stuff of music hall jokes, but for competitors and enthusiasts alike the prospect of a wet weekend raised dark memories of Easter seven years earlier when Donington Park hosted the European Grand Prix for the first and only time.

Moreover, while British race fans are a hardy breed, well-seasoned in standing for endless hours on muddy banks while awaiting the start of the show, the prospect of Bernie Ecclestone's celebrity guests soiling their Guccis was enough to send two industrial street cleaners to polish the tarmac outside the exclusive paddock club, where tickets cost around $2000 for the weekend, on the first day of sodden practice .

"Let's be clear about this," said Eddie Jordan. "No racing team wants to bring guests and sponsors to any venue if the weather is not conducive to what our business is about.

"The reason we go to Australia and Brazil in March is to chase the (most suitable) weather, so it is hazardous to be coming to Silverstone in late April.

"But those of us whose racing careers developed in this part of the world know that the weather can be precarious in even July and August, so to hope for fine weather here in April is asking for a miracle."

For his part, Michael Schumacher arrived at Silverstone dejected by the weather, but happy in the knowledge that the circuit authorities had made track improvements following Ricardo Zonta's spectacular 180mph accident during testing the previous week.

"Every circuit tries to make things as smooth as possible for us," he said, "but inevitably there are little bumps that they don't always see in the same way as we do. The tyre barrier (at the point Zonta crashed) has been slightly raised and we made a couple of other changes at the Bridge and Becketts corners."

Meanwhile, while British Formula 1 newcomer Jenson Button continued at the centre of fevered attention in the paddock, his employer Frank Williams was inscrutably non-commital about whether or not he will be retaining the 20-year-old's services for the 2001 season.

"He has exceeded our expectations," said Williams. "We don't have to reach any decision today, or prematurely. From what we have seen of him in the cockpit, he is exceptionally calm and is available to us if we should so choose."

The 2000 British Grand Prix was certainly one to forget, with TV images of spectators' cars being hauled, axle-deep in mud from saturated car parks, painting an acutely embarrassing picture of a sport which looked chaotically organised and unprofessional.

Ecclestone, who many blamed for the date rescheduling which resulted in this debacle, amazed F1 insiders when he performed an apparent volte-face by saying: "Silverstone have made a big effort which they haven't done in the past and it (the Grand Prix) should stay here."

He added; "I hope Brands Hatch and Silverstone can get their act together and sort things out. They could do it in ten minutes if they wanted to."

Ecclestone also called for the government to invest more in sport in general and motor racing in particular. Many saw this as the only realistic way in which the future of the British Grand Prix can be guaranteed on a long-term basis.

"Motor racing brings a huge amount of income into Britain, so perhaps the government might like to consider helping with support as other countries do," he said.

He clearly had in mind the new state-of-the-art Sepang circuit at Kuala Lumpur, funded by the Malaysian government and its national fuel company Petronas, and the way in which the Victoria government fund the Australian Grand Prix at Melbourne.

Therein lay the snag. Even prior to taking a dramatic loss on Sunday's race, Silverstone was baulking at Ecclestone's planned price hike for 2002.

The BRDC was facing a bill of around $1m in reimbursement costs for those angry and frustrated fans who were unable to gain access to the muddy spectator areas on Sunday.

For them, Ecclestone's conciliatory words over the weekend to the effect that the track deserved to keep the British Grand Prix beyond the next year's expiry of its current contract had not materially changed the situation.

The BRDC defended its position by pointing out that it is a commercial operation which stands or falls by the strength of its own business ingenuity and has the benefit of no such subsidy.

"If we signed up for the new five-year deal – and then incurred a loss like we've incurred this year – then the whole future of Silverstone could be jeopardised," said BRDC director Howden Ganley.

Fair enough, but such even-tempered reality cut little ice in the mud-soaked Silverstone car parks on Sunday evening. "All I know is that when I walk into Melbourne's Albert Park circuit, I think 'what a nice place,'" said an Australian fan struggling to leave on Sunday. "I don't think 'oh, the cost of this is coming out of my pocket.' And all I know is that I think Silverstone is a dump."

The FIA, for one, didn't mince its words. It immediately announced that the British Grand Prix would be dropped from the 2001 calendar unless the organisers could satisfy it that it would address and rectify these organisational shortcomings.

Definite inclusion on the calendar would now depend on confirmation from FIA safety delegate Charlie Whiting that changes proposed to the procedures in the Silverstone race control have been implemented and that satisfactory plans must be submitted to show how the circuit and police authorities will ensure that there will be no repetition of the traffic problems which arose in 2000.

Furthermore, the FIA is demanding a report detailing how ticket-holding spectators who could not enter the circuit have been compensated. This last point particularly refers to the crowds who were turned away from Saturday qualifying after the promoters closed the sodden public car parks in a last-ditch attempt to improve conditions for race day.

However, the Motor Sports Association, Britain's national club, and Silverstone's owners, the British Racing Drivers' Club, both felt that they could meet the FIA's exacting requirements in time for the next World Council meeting on 4 October 2000.

"The MSA, Silverstone and the BRDC accept the conclusion of the hearing of the FIA World Council in Warsaw today," said a spokesperson.

"The conditions attached to next year's Grand Prix are indeed those which Silverstone would have considered in any event. All provisions will be complied with in good time for the World Motor Sport Council meeting in October." The promoters duly aided the future of their race by proposing an unprecedented 5m pound gamble which has been accepted by the sport's governing body.

Octagon Motorsports offered to lodge that sum with the FIA as a guarantee of their confidence that they have solved the traffic access problems which have blighted the last two Grands Prix at Silverstone, leaving thousands of spectators fuming in their cars for miles around.

Further details and terms of what was described as a "performance bond" would also be agreed between Octagon and the FIA's lawyers. If the arrangements for the race do not come up to the expected standards, then the money could be forfeited.

However, it has now emerged that even Tony Blair was sufficiently moved by the seriousness of the situation to put in a reassuring phone call to FIA president Max Mosley in advance of the World Motor Sport Council meeting in Monte Carlo where the future of the race was decided.

It was a gesture of support which reflected the crucial importance of the British Grand Prix not only as the country's biggest stand-alone sporting event, but also the adverse impact on the motor racing industry which cancelling the race might have had.

In addition to persuasive support from the prime minister's office, Tessa Jowell and minister for sport Richard Cabourn all brought their influence to bear on the FIA. Mosley also received calls from the chief constables of Thames Valley and Northamptonshire, assuring him that traffic-flow arrangements for next year's race would be up to the required standards.

Jackie Stewart, who by now had succeeded Hesketh as president of the BRDC, worked hard behind the scenes using his connections to lobby the politicians.

"We have had unprecedented help from the government on this," he said. "I was relatively confident even before the meeting at Monaco that the FIA was going to receive the reassurance about the race that it needed – and some of this was directed from the very top."

Stewart, who won two British Grand Prix victories at Silverstone for the Tyrrell team during his own racing career, added: "I am very pleased this matter has now been resolved for Silverstone. I think Octagon and everybody else involved in this worked hard to satisfy the FIA's requirements."

However, the governing body also accepted a confidential report from the Motor Sports Association, Britain's national authority, that there had in fact been "material and noticeable" improvements to the traffic flow in 2001 and that the plans in hand for 2002 "address every aspect required from Grand Prix organisers and more".

The 2002 race went ahead as scheduled, but there was still pressure on the event. However, Silverstone's upgrade did not seem totally to satisfy the rigorous standards of the sport's commercial rights holder Bernie Ecclestone.

Clearly vexed and in a very grumpy mood that low cloud delayed his arrival by helicopter on the morning of the race, Ecclestone slummed it by road from a nearby landing field but roundly criticised the signposting once he had arrived at the track.

Whilst acknowledging the traffic flow was much improved, he added that more needed to be done. "Generally the organisation was pretty bad in some respects," he said, "far worse than it has ever been.

"There were no signs inside the circuit and nobody seemed to know what they were doing. I did not think the public were being well looked after."

However Rob Bain, chairman of race promoters Octagon Motorsports, brushed his concerns aside. "It comes down to the fact that his helicopter couldn't land, his car got lost and he wasn't very happy," he replied firmly.

Twenty-four hours later Bain had resigned his position, although not specifically due to this frank exchange of views. Some insiders thought he was well out of it.

It was unlikely that Ecclestone had failed to grasp the significance of the British Grand Prix within the wider international motor racing infrastructure. What he seemed to want was to bounce the government into giving support to Formula 1 within the UK, just as governments elsewhere in the world had done to support such a prestige dollar-earning event.

The mathematics certainly added up in that respect. The race generated considerable income for the surrounding area. The stark reality was that the British Grand Prix annually injected over $50m into the local economy around Silverstone thanks to the influx of visitors. Yet still Ecclestone seemed inclined to ride Silverstone hard and offer them little but constant aggravation.

By the start of 2003, it was clear that Octagon had made a huge mistake in purchasing Brands Hatch Leisure under the financial terms prevailing at the time.

Interestingly, in the run-up to the start of the 2003 Formula 1 Championship season, nobody at Octagon would say anything on the record. It was quite clear that the whole business had been a ghastly mistake and they were battening down the hatches to engineer an exit strategy as quickly as they possibly could.

Then, in March 2003, Ecclestone struck again. Having been asked by the media for a comment on Octagon's growing dilemma, he blamed the BRDC for all the problems surrounding the British Grand Prix.

"If the British Grand Prix disappears from Britain, it will be because no one can afford Silverstone's rent," he said in an astonishing outburst which was demonstrably just not correct.

"The BRDC should run the race and be the promoter. We did a contract with them that was very cheap for them to run.

"Once, the idea was to sell Silverstone. But they decided not to do it – and got someone to rent it out."

Octagon's motor racing business was currently valued at around $72m – less than half its purchase price from BHL.

"The contract is guaranteed by Interpublic," said Ecclestone, who denied that he wanted to take over the race. "But if no one wants to run the race, then there won't be a British Grand Prix."

It fell to Martin Brundle, the BRDC's chairman, to reply that Ecclestone was, in effect, talking nonsense. He slammed back at Ecclestone over this unfathomable continuing criticism and apparent animosity towards the British Grand Prix.

"It is clear for anyone to see that Bernie seems to have been trying hard to destabilise the British Grand Prix, Silverstone and the BRDC," he said.

"Jackie Stewart (the BRDC president) and I have been saying that we're going to lose the British Grand Prix and it's becoming a very real issue. The BRDC has continued to be proactively willing to find a future solution to this issue."

For his part, Stewart was also robust in his comments, clearly sympathising with Octagon's dilemma but at the same time acknowledging that they had not been very astute in their business judgement.

"You wouldn't see Warren Buffet doing things like this," he said. "They over-invested and didn't have the management team to handle it. Clearly Octagon did inadequate due diligence when they started on this programme.

"That said, we have received assurances from the highest level within Interpublic that there is no question of them doing anything but honouring that contract. It has been reported that they wish to exit their motorsport strategy in a timely manner and I accept that."

Despite this, the BRDC issued a statement on 17 March 2003 saying: "Whilst we are aware of general statements, at no time have the BRDC been formally notified by Octagon/Interpublic of their intention to sell their commercial rights at Silverstone or any other motor racing entities.

"We have knowledge of the Octagon/Interpublic contract to promote the British Grand Prix, the cost of which, over the contract period, significantly exceeds that of the lease costs for Silverstone, its circuits and businesses.

"As a small not-for-profit organisation, the BRDC does not have the financial depth to operate an annual Formula 1 contract under the present terms and conditions on offer from Formula One Management and particularly without the government support which exists in most other host countries.

"The BRDC, as custodian as Silverstone, is best able to support British motorsport and emerging British drivers with a steady income stream and we look forward to a long and successful relationship with our operating tenants."

So how will it all shake out? Well, whatever they may have been saying as this book went to press, the clever money sees Interpublic cutting a deal to get out of its ongoing obligation to the BRDC on the Silverstone lease by making a handsome one-off payment. Possibly even by the time these words are published.

Octagon's contract with Ecclestone is a more tricky affair. Negotiating a release from this deal will not only be extremely costly, but it will result in Bernie becoming *de facto* rights holder to the British Grand Prix.

Then he can be expected to cut a bargain-basement deal with the BRDC to rent the circuit for a couple of weeks every year to run the British Grand Prix on his own terms.

That said, Interpublic and its subsidiaries have behaved with absolute probity and clearly have no intention of jeopardising the image of their other European business investments by reneging on any of their Formula 1 obligations.

Whatever the outcome, the British Grand Prix will survive. At the end of the day, Ecclestone may rant and rave about its facilities, castigate the owners of Silverstone and generally keep everybody dancing to his own tune.

Yet he will never be the man to cancel the British Grand Prix. He knows that every sponsor and car maker involved in the sport will rebel to a man. In fact, F1 revisionists might well even one day cast him in the role of the man who saved it.

It is even suggested in some quarters that Ecclestone could not get rid of the British Grand Prix even if he *really* wanted to. Formula

1 insiders increasingly whisper – admittedly in tones sufficiently hushed so as not to reach Bernie's eyrie in Princes Gate – that the Concorde Agreement gives the British race "protected status" alongside a handful of other prestige events on the calendar.

Yet no outsider who has had sight of the Concorde Agreement – and lived to tell the tale – will either confirm or deny this juicy morsel of information.

So what will be Bernie's reward? Adulation from Tony Blair's government with a promise of support for the race from the public purse? Probably not, particularly after the controversy over the donation to the Labour Party after the tobacco sponsorship controversy in 1997.

Ennoblement, even, for his services to motorsport over more than a generation? Well, perhaps. Formula 1 insiders are divided as to whether Ecclestone would relish such an acknowledgement or dismiss it as a meaningless trinket.

Yet don't bet against it. The day could come when Sir Bernard and Lady Ecclestone, dressed in their best bib and tuckers, ride away through the gates of Buckingham Palace in some suitably lavish barouche.

It may seem an unlikely dawn to some within the sport, but stranger things have happened in the wacky world of Formula 1. A world which Mr E might not have created, but which he certainly transformed beyond all recognition.